LifeCaps Presents:

Selfridge:

The Life and Times of Harry Gordon Selfridge

By Fergus Mason

BOOKCAPS

BookCaps™ Study Guides

www.bookcaps.com

Selfridge, Gordon

Cover Image © Michael Gray - Fotolia.com

Table of Contents

About LifeCaps

LifeCaps is an imprint of BookCaps™ Study Guides. With each book, a lesser known or sometimes forgotten life is recapped. We publish a wide array of topics (from baseball and music to literature and philosophy), so check our growing catalogue regularly (**www.bookcaps.com**) to see our newest books.

Introduction

Just for a moment try to put every shopping trip you've ever made out of your head. Imagine a different world. Imagine that all the goods for sale are locked away in cabinets and to handle them, or even to examine them closely, you need to ask a shop assistant to open it up for you. Imagine that within seconds of entering a store a floorwalker approaches you and asks if you're planning to buy something – then, when you say "I'm just looking," rudely tells you to leave. Imagine any attempt to return faulty or unsuitable goods being met with ridicule, obstruction or a flat refusal to help you.

Until the late 19th century people didn't have to imagine that; it was reality. For anyone alive today a visit to the average store back then would convince you that they didn't really *want* to sell you anything. The idea of customer service was an alien one. Stores sold things. If you wanted to buy them, fine. If you didn't they weren't really interested. Browsing was strongly discouraged and impulse buys were almost unheard of. Shopping was something you did when you had to. It certainly wasn't something anyone enjoyed.

Then, in the late 1880s, one man came along and changed all that. He set out to make shopping fun, and to make the customer feel valued. He spread the idea that it was fine to just look around. He also introduced many of the concepts we now take for granted – the Christmas retail season, wedding gift lists, in-store entertainment and even the bargain basement. His name was Harry Gordon Selfridge.

Harry Selfridge grew up in small-town America after the Civil War, and tried his hand at a variety of careers before taking a job at one of Chicago's leading wholesalers. After a successful career in management he moved to the retail side of the business and instantly went to work on revolutionizing the way it worked.

What he'd accomplished by the age of fifty was more than enough to be proud of, but Selfridge wasn't content. Next he set himself the challenge of moving to London and founding a new, unique department store that would turn out be the prototype for every one that followed. That store is still in business more than a century later and it still bears his name.

For decades the name of Harry Selfridge has been almost forgotten, but a recent TV series from ITV and PBS has pushed his name back into the limelight. He's almost as well known today as he was on a wet March day in 1909 when his new store opened its doors to admit a flood of excited Londoners. TV drama is TV drama, though, and the story it tells is as manufactured as the image Selfridge created for himself so long ago. There's a lot more to it than what you can see on the screen – the struggle, the disappointments and above all the family who helped him on his way to success. *Mr. Selfridge* told the fairy tale version of the story; here's the real thing.

Chapter 1: The Young Entrepreneur

Anyone who's ever moved to a new town knows what a challenge it can be. Starting off in an unfamiliar house, finding the best stores, getting to know new neighbors… it can be an intimidating prospect. So just imagine how it must have felt to the pioneers who moved west across America in the 19th century. They were heading into the unknown, not just moving to a new town but trying to establish one. To do that takes an incredible level of determination, which means it takes a special kind of person. Even when a settlement began to grow and take shape moving there was definitely not for the faint hearted. Many new towns grew fitfully for a few years then faded away; others prospered. It often took decades to be sure which way a town was going to go, so moving to a new settlement took real courage.

David P. Mapes had built a career hauling cut timber down the rivers of New York state on one of the new steam-powered riverboats. He was successful enough to get elected to the State Assembly in 1831, but it seems he wanted a bigger challenge. In 1845 he moved to Wisconsin, and sometime between then and 1846 he negotiated a land purchase from state land secretary John Scott Horner. It was an expensive undertaking because the purchase came with several conditions; within a year of taking over the land he had to build both a flour mill and an inn, and then run the inn himself for twelve months. In return he could use the water power from the mill's wheel for his own purposes, and would own every alternate lot in the new town. Horner also wanted the right to name the settlement, and as he was the one who controlled land allocation Mapes couldn't refuse. He did manage to impose some conditions of his own though; the name shouldn't be a personal one, it had to be unique in the USA, it wasn't to be a Native American name and it must be short. If the land secretary had any dreams of calling the town Hornerville they ended right there. Instead he settled on Ripon, after his English ancestors' hometown in Yorkshire.

In February 1849 Mapes moved to his new land with his two sons and their families, and began clearing the ground.[i] Within a year, as specified, the mill was running and the Ripon House Inn was open for business. Soon families started moving into the vacant plots and the town began to grow. It was an uphill struggle at first, because Ripon wasn't on a navigable river or close to the growing railway network, but it was surrounded by good prairie land and Mapes worked hard to attract settlers. On March 20, 1854 a new anti-slavery party was founded at a meeting in the Ripon schoolhouse and decided to call itself the Republican Party.[ii] In case that wasn't enough to bring in more people, Mapes gave away lots in the town on condition that the new owners made specified improvements to the land. Sometime in the early 1850s Robert and Lois Selfridge took up this offer and moved to Ripon. With them went their two children, Robert Jr. and Charles.

The couple's third son, Henry Gordon "Harry" Selfridge, was born in Ripon on January 11, 1856 (not 1858 as many people believe).[iii] Robert Oliver Selfridge was looking for an opportunity that would let him bring up his young family, and obviously he thought he could find it in this small new town in rural Wisconsin. Within months of Harry's birth, however, something new came along: he had the chance to buy the general store in Jackson, Michigan. Robert didn't hesitate; showing the same willingness to start again that had brought him to Ripon in the first place he uprooted his family again and moved 250 miles southeast to take over the store.

Five years later the store was a successful business, but now politics intervened. The Republican Party had come a long way from its first meeting in the Ripon schoolhouse, and by 1858 it was the dominant political force in most of the northern states. On November 6, 1860 the party's presidential candidate, Abraham Lincoln, won a four-way race to become the 16th President of the United States. The election triggered a rapid slide towards war.

The 1860 Republican platform had played down the slavery issue, causing outrage among the party's hardliners. Lincoln promised not to legislate against slavery in the states, but did hint at abolishing it in the territories. It was too moderate a position for many in his own party, but nowhere near moderate enough for the southern states where slavery was a major part of the agricultural industry. A group of state governors began planning secession and in February 1861 – just days before Lincoln was inaugurated as president on March 4 – seven states announced that they were leaving the USA to establish a confederacy. On April 12, Confederate forces attacked US forces in Fort Sumter, a fortress that controlled the entrance to Charleston Harbor, and Lincoln called for the states to provide 75,000 militia to suppress the Confederate Army. That request pushed four more states into joining the Confederacy and the war, limited up to that point, began to explode out of control. Within months, tens of thousands of men in both north and south had volunteered to join up and fight, and the Union Army started to swell from its peacetime strength of just 16,000 men towards a final total of over two million. One of those who volunteered was Robert Selfridge.

As far as the war itself went, Robert did fine; he became an officer in the Union Army and was eventually promoted to major. When the Confederacy surrendered in May 1865, he was demobilized along with hundreds of thousands more veterans, but while most of them returned home, Robert, for reasons unknown, decided not to. Instead he simply vanished, leaving no trace beyond a record of honorable discharge.[iv] Lois chose not to tell her sons what had happened; instead she told them that their father had been killed in action, a claim that Harry often repeated to newspapers through his life.[v] It was only much later that he learned the truth. Dead or vanished, however, Robert Selfridge was gone and either way the effect on Lois and her family was the same; she was left alone to bring up three young boys.

As much of a struggle as raising three children on her own must have been, it must still have been a shocking blow when Robert Jr. and Charles both died within a few months of the war's end. That left her with just Harry, but without her husband's army pay or the income from the now-sold general store she was still desperate for money. Finally she found a job as a schoolteacher, which gave her a small but regular income. At first she supplemented it by selling hand-painted greeting cards; eventually she worked her way up and became headmistress of the local high school.

In those early years after the war, it was a constant struggle to make ends meet, and at the age of ten Harry started to make his own contribution. He found work in the village store, delivering newspapers and collecting payments from customers; that brought in an extra $1.50 a week.[vi] Two years later he started working part-time at Leonard Field's dry goods store. When he was thirteen, he and a friend from school, Peter Loomis, began producing a monthly magazine for boys. Despite their age the two ran it as a proper business and even made money from selling advertising space. The experience gave young Harry a taste of life as an entrepreneur. It wasn't enough of an income, though, and soon he began looking for a full time job. Aged 14 he was offered a place as a clerk at a local bank, and left school to take it up – few states had compulsory schooling laws at the time and Michigan wasn't among them, but even where school was mandatory the leaving age was 14.

Selfridge doesn't seem to have enjoyed the bank job very much – after the thrill of running his own small business with Loomis it's hard to blame him – but he had other plans. His ambition now was to become an officer in the US Navy, and that meant going through the United States Naval Academy at Annapolis. After four years at the Naval Academy successful midshipmen graduate with a degree and a commission, so competition has always been stiff. In the early 1870s it was even more so; the navy was being cut savagely in the aftermath of the Civil War and there were few vacancies for new officers. The Class of 1868 graduated only 25 officers and the total number of cadets at the time was less than 200. It took determination to get in, and physical standards were also high. Harry was charming and persuasive and probably had little trouble with the interview process, but when it came to his physical examination it was a different story. With so few vacancies, the Academy could afford to tighten its already strict standards, and there was no room for flexibility for those who didn't quite match up. One of those standards was a minimum height limit, and Harry Selfridge was just short of it – some sources say by only a quarter of an inch. That was enough for Annapolis to reject his application. It was a crushing disappointment for Selfridge, and left him with a lifelong sensitivity about his short stature.

After failing to get a place at Annapolis, Selfridge had to look for a new career. He initially returned to Jackson and found a job with a local furniture factory, working as a bookkeeper. Four months later, the company went out of business and Harry had to move on again. He found another bookkeeper's job, this time at an insurance office in Grand Rapids.

Selfridge's big break came in 1876 when Leonard Field, the owner of the dry goods store where he'd worked for a while, agreed to write him a letter of recommendation to Marshall Field. Marshall Field, who'd moved to Chicago from Massachusetts the year Harry was born, had worked for a Chicago dry goods chain for several years. Then in 1865 he and a colleague, Levi Leiter, bought out P. Palmer & Co., a rival store, and went into business for themselves. Three years later they moved the store into an impressive new building on State and Washington built by its original owner, Potter Palmer, who had moved into real estate. Field & Leiter, as it was called at the time, now sold a hugely expanded range of goods across six floors. Only three years later, the building was destroyed in the Great Chicago Fire of 1871, but the employees managed to save most of the merchandise before the building erupted into flames. Weeks later, Field & Leiter reopened in temporary premises, then moved back to State Street in 1873.

In 1876, when Selfridge applied for a job there, Marshall Field operated both the increasingly popular retail store and a much larger wholesale division. Selfridge was taken on in the stock department of the wholesale business, which supplied merchandise to many smaller stores throughout the Midwest and the western USA. As a junior stock boy his duties included breaking down bulk consignments of goods as they arrived at the warehouse and transferring them to the stock shelves from where the orders division would collect and ship them. It would have been hard work, hauling boxes around the huge building on a cart, and the turnover rate among employees was high. However, that meant there were opportunities for anyone who was prepared to stick with it. Harry Selfridge was prepared to stick with it, and he gradually advanced through the wholesale division.

Another fire destroyed the retail store in 1877, but by 1879 it was operating again in a new, even larger building on the State and Washington site. In 1881, Field bought out Leiter's share of the business and renamed the store Marshall Field & Co. It would remain as Chicago's leading department store until Macy's bought it out in 2006. Through this period the retail store continued to grow in importance. By 1887, while the wholesale side still brought in six times the income, the big store was the best known part of the business. That year the wholesale side of the company moved into a new seven-story Romanesque building that took up an entire block. It was much larger than the previous location and needed a bigger staff, so again there were promotion opportunities for the existing employees. Selfridge, by now a senior manager in the bulk stock department, was probably expecting another advancement. As it turned out he got it, but it moved him onto a new career path.

As the wholesale division moved into its new premises, Selfridge was told that instead of moving with it he was being transferred to the retail store as its new director – he would be in charge of that whole part of the business. It was a significant move, given that the share of Marshall Field's total profits generated by retail had been slowly rising for several years. Field himself clearly saw it as playing an even more important role in the future, and it says a lot for his opinion of Harry that he put him in charge of it at this point, when the wholesale store itself was going through a major expansion.

Chapter 2: Reinventing Retail

When Harry Selfridge took over the retail arm of Marshall Field he was 31 years old and he'd been with the company for ten years. He'd worked his way up through what was still the more profitable side of the company and carried out a wide range of jobs, from his initial time as a stock boy to managing the flow of orders heading out to retailers across two-thirds of the USA. However, all his jobs with the company had been out of the public eye, and he hadn't been dealing face to face with customers.

Of course, as head of the entire store there was no real reason for him to deal with customers if he didn't want to. He had a general manager and a whole team of floor managers who could insulate him from the actual business of selling things to people. If he'd spent his days in his office, passing instructions down the chain and listening to the feedback that came back up it, nobody at Marshall Field would have thought any the worse of him. But that's not what he chose to do.

It looks as though moving to the retail side unlocked a buried potential in Harry. His only experience of facing customers directly had been long ago, as a boy working in the store back in Jackson. Now he had the opportunity to do it again, if he wanted, in a much grander setting. He threw himself into it enthusiastically. Instead of staying in his spacious office running the store remotely he spent every minute he could walking the sales floors, watching how his staff handled their jobs and – more importantly – watching the customers and how they spent their time inside the store.

Marshall Field had a lot in common with a modern department store in terms of its layout and what was available, but the way staff acted toward customers was very different – and in ways that wouldn't be anywhere close to acceptable today. Advertising standards were much looser and sellers could get away with what, now, would be seen as illegal misrepresentations. They often did get away with it, too. The law regarding sales in the USA was ruled by the principle of *caveat emptor* – "Let the buyer beware" – following an 1817 ruling by the Supreme Court in the *Laidlaw v. Organ* case. In 1815, Hector M. Organ had bought fifty tons of tobacco from trader Peter Laidlaw, and while they were drawing up the contract, Laidlaw asked Organ if he knew anything that might affect tobacco prices over the next few days. Organ said he didn't, but he was lying; his brother had told him that morning that the USA and Britain had just signed a treaty to end the War of 1812. During the war, the Royal Navy had blockaded the US coast, crippling trade and slashing the price of tobacco by half. Hours after Organ drove away with his wagonloads of tobacco, the news broke across the USA and the price soared. Laidlaw tried to get the goods back on the grounds that Organ had misled him, but first the District Court of Louisiana and then the US Supreme Court ruled that Organ had not been obliged to disclose relevant information.[vii]

Although in this case it was the seller who had suffered (making it technically a case of *caveat venditor*), both retailers and wholesalers throughout the USA embraced the principle enthusiastically. About the only limit the courts placed on their actions was that sellers couldn't hide defects in their products, but they certainly didn't have to tell anyone about them. As the legal definition of "defect" included products that were completely unfit for their advertised purpose it was a minefield for shoppers, and they had very little chance of redress if they ended up being misled.

With such a free-for-all, and virtual immunity from legal action, it's perhaps natural that retail staff felt superior when dealing with customers and often let it show. If a customer did complain about a product or service they were usually fobbed off with excuses, with the *caveat emptor* argument available as an almost unbeatable weapon of last resort. It was what American shoppers were used to and, as Marshall Field's growing retail business showed, they mostly accepted it. Harry Selfridge watched and learned, and he soon decided that even if people were willing to put up with the retail industry the way it was, the store he was now running could – and should – do better.

What Selfridge set out to do was to fundamentally change the way retail staff and customers interacted. Instead of making people feel like they were barely tolerated in the store, a nuisance who disrupted the smooth running of the place, he told his staff to make them feel welcome. The first step was to revolutionize the way customer enquiries and complaints were handled. The service staff was ordered to stop trying to brush off customers who were unhappy with something they'd purchased; instead, their complaints were to be carefully and sympathetically listened to, and wherever possible, acted on. To help educate staff in what he expected of them, a new slogan was placed at the heart of the store's philosophy: "The customer is always right".

Of course the customer *isn't* always right; sometimes – often – they're spectacularly wrong, and anyone who works in retail has a store of funny stories about rude, mistaken or clueless customers.[viii] What Selfridge had realized, however, was that even when they are wrong it's usually just an honest misunderstanding, and that by treating them sympathetically staff could avoid arguments and ill feeling. If a customer tried to get a refund on a faulty product and was sent packing by a manager they would be resentful, and there was a good chance that next time they wanted something they'd go to a different store. On the other hand, if the staff were friendly and helpful it would leave people with a good impression of the store, and they'd be more likely to come back. After all, most complaints could be resolved without actually costing anything – refunding a sale usually meant the store got its goods back and could sell them again – and any losses that did occur would be offset by the higher chance of having that customer come back in the future.

History doesn't record whether the "customer is always right" slogan was coined by Selfridge or by Marshall Field himself, but it certainly fit with the ideas Selfridge was bringing to his new job. His aim was to make shopping at the store an enjoyable experience that people would feel enthusiastic about, and he was constantly trying out new tricks to make that happen. Other large stores, first in Chicago and then across the USA (an early one was the Philadelphia-based Wanamaker's) soon saw what was happening at Marshall Field and started to rejuvenate their own customer relations, but Selfridge was out in front of them and he had no intention of giving up his lead. The next innovation at Marshall Field was pure Selfridge, and it's still with us today.

For most retailers the weeks before Christmas are the most important part of the year. Today, department store takings in the USA are 50 per cent higher in December than in November. For other retail sectors the increase is even greater – 100 per cent in bookstores, 170 per cent for jewelers.[ix] In the 1880s the increase wasn't anywhere near as large as it is now, because gift-giving was a smaller part of the Christmas tradition, but it was still significant. Selfridge believed that by whipping up some enthusiasm among his customers he could boost sales; the question was how to do that. Most retailers didn't do much beyond getting in stocks of seasonal goods and putting up a few tired decorations, perhaps including the latest craze imported from Britain: a Christmas tree.

Anyone with a calendar could work out how many days remained until Christmas, but Selfridge decided to zero in on the days when they could visit his store. Sunday trading is now routine in most US states, although local "blue laws" might still impose restrictions, but that's not always been the case. In 1887, almost all stores were firmly closed on a Sunday, including Marshall Field. The same applied to public holidays like Thanksgiving. Selfridge figured out that by totaling up the number of days the store would be open he could generate the feeling of a countdown, reminding shoppers that their opportunities to buy Christmas gifts – plus decorations, food items and other seasonal items – were limited and steadily ticking away. That led him to develop a new slogan; soon it was appearing in Marshall Fields adverts on billboards and in local newspapers, as well as on huge banners above the entrances and display windows of the store itself. Hurry up and shop, they subconsciously urged passersby, because there are "Only X Shopping Days Until Christmas".

Under Selfridge's dynamic leadership the Marshall Field retail store went from strength to strength. More innovations were introduced. Goods were taken down from high shelves and displayed at waist height on tables and counters, creating a more friendly and inviting appearance. The spartan ladies' cloakrooms were remodeled, and a store restaurant – the first in Chicago – was opened. Previously, the display windows had been dark at night; now they were kept illuminated so passersby could see what was on display at any time.[x] Those displays were far more appealing, too, with more naturally posed mannequins displaying complimentary items. These were all Selfridge's ideas, the product of an energy that earned him the nickname "Mile-a-minute Harry" among the store's staff. At the same time, he was also pursuing his private life, and his success there was just as great as what he'd achieved at Marshall Field.

Chapter 3: Mrs. Selfridge

The first member of the Buckingham family to make a mark in the New World was Alvah Buckingham. He was born in March 1791, at Ballston Springs, New York, and few details of his parents are known. It's reasonable to assume from their surname that they or their immediate ancestors were from England. When Alvah was a young boy the family moved to Cooperstown, then in 1799 struck out to the west. By 1802, they were settled in Athens County, in what would later become the township of Carthage. The growing settlement had a school and the Buckinghams could afford to send Alvah and his two older brothers there; education was far from universal at the time. Outside of school they helped on the family farm and hunted in the surrounding woods. From what's known about society at the time we can guess that the oldest brother would have taken over the farm in time, but the other two had different ideas. In 1812 Alvah and his brother Ebenezer moved to Putnam, near Zanesville, and set up a grain shipping business on the banks of the Muskingum River. The Muskingum flows into the Ohio River at Marietta, and the Ohio in turn empties into the Mississippi, so E. Buckingham & Co. could ship the grain they bought to a huge expanse of the expanding nation.

Unfortunately, Ebenezer Buckingham died in 1832. Alvah reorganized the company and changed the name to A. Buckingham & Co, and took on a partner named Solomon Sturges to help him run the business. In 1845 there was another reorganization; the old company was dissolved and a new one, Buckingham & Sturges, formed. They helped build the first grain elevator in Chicago in 1851 and opened branches in New York and Toledo, which were run by Buckingham's oldest sons. One of these, Benjamin Buckingham, later took over the firm's business in Chicago, which by the late 1850s was immense. In addition to their own shipping and storage business, they had a contract with the Illinois Central Railroad to do all their grain warehousing for the next ten years,[xi] and an increasing number of other major contracts throughout the East Coast and Midwest.

Benjamin Buckingham and his brother Philo steadily took on larger roles in running the Chicago operations, and thanks to their considerable wealth, also became notable figures in upper-class Chicago society. Benjamin married another member of that society, Martha Euretta Potwin, and on July 5, 1960 their first daughter was born. Rosalie Amelia Buckingham was brought up from the start in a way that suited her for life among the industrial aristocracy, but sadly when she was only four years old, her father died suddenly. That was a tragedy, but in financial terms at least the family was secure; Rose, her younger sister Anna and their mother all inherited large sums from Benjamin, more than adequate to let them live in the same grand style as they had enjoyed so far.

The rich at the time were educated at home or in private schools, and a tour of Europe was seen as an essential part of a girl's development. Between 1873 and 1879 Rose, Anna and Martha made several trips to various European countries, where the girls studied languages and music.[xii] She may also have studied business, because a few years later she started investing in high-end Chicago real estate. In 1883, she bought a row of plots along South Harper Avenue in the Hyde Park neighborhood, which would become part of the city in 1889, with the intention of building a row of luxury houses. To help with this she went looking for an architect and found one of Chicago's leading building experts, Solon Spencer Beman. Beman was a controversial figure in the city, having designed a planned workers' community for the Pullman Railroad Company, but his talent was never in doubt. He later went on to create Chicago's famous Grand Central Station. Now Rose asked him to start designing houses on several plots along her property.

While Beman set to work on what would become known as the Rosalie Villas, Rose herself went travelling again. From 1884 to 1888 she and her family spent time in Europe and the Middle East. Their catalogue of destinations was far more extensive than most wealthy Americans visited, and included Britain, Germany, the Scandinavian countries, Russia, Turkey, Egypt and the Holy Land. In the fall of 1888, Rose returned to Chicago and, in addition to re-entering the social scene, brought herself up to date on the progress of her building project. Sometime later that year she met Harry Selfridge at a function and a relationship began to develop.

By now, Rose was 28 years old, and by the standards of the time she'd already left it quite late to find a husband. Most women of her social class were presented as debutantes in their late teens or early twenties, attending a series of organized social events where they would meet "suitable" young men, and the majority of them were married by the time they were 22 or 23 years old. Rose was still single, and there is some evidence she was sensitive about this; when she applied for a new passport in 1888 she gave her year of birth as 1866, subtracting six years from her real age. Her age wasn't a problem for Selfridge, though – at 30 he was past the normal marriage age himself, so he and Rose were a good match.

Selfridge's career was also progressing well. On January 1, 1890 Marshall Field made him a junior partner in the firm, hugely increasing both his income and his status. He was no longer a mere employee, but part-owner of a major business.

Harry Selfridge and Rose Buckingham married in Chicago's Central Church on November 11, 1890. They didn't find a home of their own immediately; instead they moved in with Rose's sister, Anna Buckingham Chandler and her husband. Lois Selfridge also moved in; she would live with the couple all through their married life, an arrangement that was quite common across all social classes at the time if one spouse's mother was widowed. In this case, both their fathers were dead, and Martha Buckingham was already living there. The newlyweds didn't plan to stay there in the long term, however; they soon began looking for a home of their own.

By this time, Rose's property in Hyde Park was fully developed, with a number of other prominent architects including Beman having designed houses there. The area had become a planned development in a beautifully landscaped setting, with over 40 villas and cottages. Building a home there was an option, but they decided against it. Meanwhile, they set about increasing the size of their family. Sadly, their first son, Chandler, died shortly after he was born in 1891, but four more children followed over the next ten years. Rosalie Jr. was born in 1893, Violette in 1897, Gordon Jr. in 1900 and Beatrice in 1901.[xiii]

The Selfridges now had a secure place in Chicago society, but they weren't confining themselves to the city. Shortly after they married they began looking for a country home as well. They settled on Lake Geneva in Walworth County, Wisconsin; with easy access from Chicago by train this small town had become a popular vacation resort for the city's wealthier inhabitants, many of whom had built homes there, and the couple had been spending their summers there since their marriage. In fact their first son, Chandler, was buried in the resort's churchyard. It was a place they both loved.

At that time most of the lake frontage hadn't yet been bought up, and Harry managed to buy a plot. It was a vacant plot of course, but he already knew what he wanted to put on it. Chicago's biggest event of 1893 was the World's Fair held in the city, which had attracted more than 27 million visitors. It featured nearly 200 buildings built by representatives from 46 countries, many of them built to show off traditional architectural styles, and a huge range of other attractions. The first Ferris wheel was built there, part of a carnival area centered on the Midway Plaisance park – that's why the sideshow area of a carnival is now called the midway in the USA. The first commercial movie theater was part of the fair, as was the first moving walkway. What had caught the eye of the Selfridges, however, was one of the national pavilions. It had been built by the island nation of Ceylon, now Sri Lanka, in a traditional style. Along with most of the other buildings, it was scheduled for demolition when the fair ended but instead Harry bought it, had it dismantled, then shipped it to Lake Geneva and had it rebuilt on his plot. It quickly became known as Ceylon Co

urt.[xiv]

As much as the Selfridges liked their lakeside home, it was only a short-term solution. Like most of the other temporary buildings it was built from a compound called "staff," a mix of cement, plaster and jute fibers that formed a sort of early drywall, and it wouldn't survive many seasons in the Midwestern climate. If they wanted to have a permanent home by the lake – and they did – they would need to build a more durable one.

There was another vacant plot right next to Ceylon Court, a large one with 300 feet of shore. Harry managed to buy that one too, and on it he had a house built. It was a remarkable structure, both in design and appearance. From the outside it was a large English-style mock Tudor mansion, with the ground floor built from local stone and the upper floors in timber and white plaster. Underneath the traditional appearance, however, was a steel structural frame; it was probably the first example of fireproof construction used in a private home.[xv] As a tribute to his wife, roses were used throughout the property as a decorative theme; even the iron fence posts that surrounded it each had a rose cast into the metal. It was a beautiful and luxurious house and both of the Selfridges loved it. As a name, they gave it a composite of their own names: Harrose Hall.

Harrose Hall was completed in 1899 and instantly became a favorite of the whole family. For decades afterwards, the couple and their children would return to the house every chance they had, even if it meant travelling an extra thousand miles just to spend a day there. Until it was finally demolished in 1975, it remained one of the most spectacular and comfortable houses in Lake Geneva.

The same year Harrose Hall was completed, the Selfridges finally found themselves a home of their own in Chicago. It was an imposing Victorian villa at 117 Lake Shore Drive (now 1430 North Lake Shore Drive) that had been built in 1890 for an elderly widow. She had died in 1898 and the house subsequently came on the market. The Selfridges managed to buy it for $100,000. At the time the average cost of a family home in the USA was less than $5,000.

By the turn of the century, Selfridge was finally running out of things to do at Marshall Field. He was a very wealthy man by this time and had huge prestige among Chicago's businessmen for the improvements he'd introduced to the retail store, improvements that were rapidly being adopted across the nation as competitors scrambled to keep up with this new way of doing things. For the moment Marshall Field was leading the industry. Now, Harry started to wonder how well he could do if he could start with a clean slate, instead of having to work within the framework of a long-established company. In 1903, he decided to find out.

In early 1904, Selfridge sold his interest in Marshall Field & Co. and used the money as startup capital for his own department store. He bought another Chicago firm, Schlesinger & Mayer, which already had a large store, and set about reshaping it in his own image. The store was closed down, completely overhauled then reopened as H.G. Selfridge & Co. The store was a success, but for some reason not a satisfying one. Only two months after opening it Selfridge sold up – at a handsome profit – to Carson Pirie Scott & Co. Still aged only 48, he retired and set out to find ways to keep himself amused. He and his family spent much of their time at Harrose Hall. Harry bought a steam yacht to sail on the lake, although he quickly grew bored with it – probably because the lake was less than eight miles long and barely a mile wide. He played golf. And, sometimes together with Rose and the children, he traveled.

Chapter 4: London

London in the 21st century is one of the world's largest, wealthiest cities. Only two US cities – New York and Los Angeles – have a larger population in their metro areas, and LA only beats it out by a few hundred thousand. More than fifteen million people live in London's sprawl. The city itself dwarfs Los Angeles and comes within 100,000 of NYC's 8.4 million people. London is also the world's second financial center after New York, and handles a more diverse range of trades. It's the most significant capital city in Europe and a major center for education. London is an important place.

And that's now. In the first decade of the 20th century it was, quite simply, a city with no equal. The British Empire was at the absolute height of its size, wealth and power. The Royal Navy dominated every one of the world's oceans, protecting a vast trade network that brought in Canadian gold, South African diamonds, Indian hardwood and Chinese silk, along with raw materials and manufactured goods from a quarter of the world's land surface. Much of that trade and the wealth it created flowed into London. The city was already immense, bigger than any other in the world; over 6.5 million people lived there, almost twice as many as in New York.[xvi] Dozens of nations followed British law and had the British monarch as head of state; dozens more were ruled directly from the Colonial Office on Whitehall, the broad street that houses the main departments of the British government. There were more local-currency millionaires in London than in the entire USA – and £1 million was worth nearly $5 million. Moscow, Istanbul and Madrid still ruled their decaying empires, Paris was the global center of fashion, Berlin's militarism was starting to tilt the European balance of power and the big US cities were fast-growing centers of business and manufacturing, but London was the world's leading city. Rose Selfridge had been there on her earlier European trips, but her husband hadn't and now he had the time and money to make up for that. In 1906 he sailed to England for a vacation and his first destination was the capital. Unsurprisingly, when he got there Harry went shopping.

London's been a good city to go shopping in for quite awhile. In fact, nobody knows exactly how long it's been one for but it's probably something over 2,000 years. The remains of Roman shops have been found[xvii] and while their stock is long gone – either cleared out by departing owners or looted by invaders – we know that the Roman Empire had a lively retail sector. Compared to most people 2,000 years ago, even a working class Roman home contained a huge range of belongings and unlike their contemporaries most Romans didn't make many of their own possessions. Instead they bought the output of slave-powered factories that shipped their goods all over the empire; any Roman town had a range of shops selling good produced hundreds, even thousands of miles away. The retail sector declined after the fall of Rome. The Saxons, who began conquering Britain in the 5th century, were stolid farmers who lived in small communities and avoided the crumbling Roman city, and the Norsemen who followed them a few centuries later didn't really seem to understand the concept of buying things – they tended to just pillage them.

By the Middle Ages, the city's retail trade was expanding again. Daily or weekly markets were held in most public squares and the streets were lined with specialty shops selling clothing, jewelry, furnishings, weapons and much more. Shops were scattered, though; there was no concept of a shopping district, and most were run out the ground floor of the owner's house. In 1565, Sir Thomas Gresham decided to change all that.

Sir Thomas was the son of Sir Richard Gresham, a prominent merchant and former Lord Mayor of London who also served as a financial adviser to King Henry VIII. As a boy, Thomas became a merchant's apprentice for eight years, working for his uncle, and then studied at the University of Cambridge. At age 24, he moved to Antwerp, working as a merchant in the family business and also acting as the king's agent. He survived three changes of monarch and became an adviser to Queen Elizabeth I, carrying out both financial and political missions for her. Then, in 1565, he proposed building a new center of commerce for London, modeled on the great exchange in Antwerp. His vision was for a place that dealt with all levels of commerce, where merchants could make deals in comfortable, professional surroundings, and crowds of shoppers would be attracted by an array of small retailers. The Royal Exchange was completed in 1571 and Queen Elizabeth opened it in person; it contained bars and coffee shops, perfumers, clothes shops and sellers of high-quality accessories. The best way to describe it is a 16th century shopping mall.

The Royal Exchange burned down – along with most of London – between September 2 and September 5, 1666. An accident in a bakery, combined with a long hot summer that had turned the city's mostly wooden buildings to tinder sparked the Great Fire, devastating almost all of the old walled city and many outlying residential areas. It's estimated that over 80 per cent of London's homes were burned out. London had been destroyed before, however, and always rises from the ruins. Within weeks, thousands of laborers and architects were hard at work building a new city, one with safer, more durable stone houses and wider streets to replace the warren of narrow lanes that had existed before. One of them, laid out along the route of an old Roman military road, soon came to be called Oxford Street.

A huge new wave of building and modernization began in the 19th century and accelerated under the young, energetic new Queen, Victoria. Streets were redeveloped with imposing multi-story stone buildings, many of which still stand. Some of them were retail premises, including department stores. The way they were distributed was strange, though. Oxford Street quickly became one of London's premier shopping locations, with a dazzling array of high class shops including the royal jeweler, Garrards. There was one omission though. London's biggest stores were scattered elsewhere: Harrods and Harvey Nichols in Knightsbridge, Fortnum & Mason in Piccadilly and Liberty on Regent Street. When Harry and Rose wandered along Oxford Street in early 1906, looking into the shop window displays as they went, they didn't see a department store. Given his experience in that area, Harry found it a conspicuous omission. Almost immediately he started wondering if he could do something about that.

Department stores are a British invention. As the Industrial Revolution gathered speed in the late 18th century, it caused huge changes in British society, starting a massive flow of people from the countryside into the growing towns. At the same time, it sparked the beginnings of a consumer society. Factory and mill workers weren't wealthy, but they still had a lot more disposable income than they'd had as farm laborers. They began to acquire more belongings and a range of shops and street markets sprang up to meet the demand. These markets were often loud, rowdy places though, and weren't attractive to the relatively new but fast-growing middle class. This group, who had even more money to spend, were looking for stores that could supply the high-quality products they were looking for in a more comfortable atmosphere. Merchants soon started looking for ways to provide this and quite soon they hit on the solution.

Harding, Howell & Co. opened on London's exclusive Pall Mall in 1796. It was laid out on one large single floor, unlike a modern department store, but its retail space was divided into four sections by partitions of glass and wood panels. One of these dealt in ladies' clothing, another in gloves and hats, while a third sold elegant clocks and home accessories. Immediately inside the entrance were furs and fashionable fans; this was an interesting placement of luxury goods, probably designed to attract as wide a range of shoppers as possible by offering a range of desirable items at a selection of prices. Whether someone entered Harding, Howell & Co. to look at an inexpensive fan or a mink coat, once they were through the door they would find plenty more to interest them. It's a principle that department stores still use today.

Harding, Howell & Co. quickly became a success and other retailers copied and expanded the concept. Kendals in Manchester had started in 1796 as a drapery business but soon expanded into multiple floors, each selling different kinds of goods, and by 1836 had taken over a second building across the street; the two were connected by a shop-lined arcade under the street. Harrods, a Knightsbridge grocery, also expanded and by the end of the 19th century the current, enormous building was under construction. Arthur Lasenby Liberty opened his eponymous store on Regent Street in 1875, in a distinctive mock-Tudor building it still occupies, pitched at the upper levels of society; its departments, split into a huge number of small display rooms, sold only the most prestigious brands. By the time the Selfridges visited London, the city had several of Europe's leading department stores; it just didn't have one on its main shopping street.

Of course Selfridge did find London's department stores, but he remained unimpressed. Perhaps because they included some of the oldest examples in the world they seemed old-fashioned compared to what Marshall Field had become. The staff showed many of the old attitudes he'd worked so hard to overcome in Chicago and while the stock was usually extremely high quality it wasn't presented anywhere near as well as it could have been. Clearly in London, shopping was still something you did when you needed something; at Marshall Field and the American stores that were following its example, it had become an enjoyable experience in its own right.

Selfridge had retired two years earlier, having made enough money to easily last a lifetime, but already he was bored. Before too long, he started contemplating the challenge of opening a new store. He knew he could do that – he'd done it with Harry G. Selfridge & Co. – but this would be a bigger task. Instead of buying an existing building and going into business for himself in a town that already knew his reputation, he would be attempting to start from scratch and revolutionize shopping in a city with its own traditions, its own established brands and its own very different way of doing things. There was a lot that could go wrong. That probably just made the challenge even more tempting.

One of the problems with London's existing department stores was their old-fashioned way of doing things. That could be dealt with using the methods he'd introduced in Chicago. The other problem was location. He believed the best place for a new store would be on Oxford Street, which attracted more shoppers than anywhere else. The older stores were scattered through the city center. That didn't matter much to someone who wanted to buy a suit from Harrods or curtain fabric from Liberty, because those people knew what they were looking for and made a trip specifically to get it. Selfridge believed that way of doing things missed a lot of potential customers, though. If a store could attract passersby with its window displays and tempt a decent percentage of them to come inside, it could generate a lot of impulse sales. For that to work it had to be in a busy location, and Oxford Street was ideal for that.

Today, the east end of Oxford Street, where it meets Tottenham Court Road, is a disappointingly generic urban area. At street level it's an identikit parade of budget cell phone dealers, ethnic fast food joints and retail chains – everything from Jessops Photography to health food brand Holland & Barrett. Keep your eyes down and it could be any street in any British town. Look up, though, and the architecture gives you a clue as to what it once was. The handsome three and four-floor buildings, built in classic Victorian style from pale stone and red brick, have weathered well. The occasional post-War intrusion replaces bomb damage – Oxford Street was bombed by the Nazis in 1940, and again by the IRA in 1973 – but mostly, once you get above the ground floor, it's a very elegant Victorian street. In most of the buildings only the ground floor is used for business; the upper levels are residential apartments. In 1906, this was very much the fashionable end of Oxford Street, and property there was very much in demand. The cost of buying and clearing a plot big enough to hold a department store was out of the question, even for Selfridge.

Instead, he started looking around the west end of the street. This area was much less fashionable for shops, which was a disadvantage, but it had its own attractions. In the west Oxford Street ends at Marble Arch, one of London's traditional landmarks. The arch itself stands at one corner of Hyde Park, which attracts many visitors, and in addition to being the end of Oxford Street it's also the end of one of London's many millionaires' rows, Park Lane. Overall, there was enough going on along the western end to guarantee a good supply of passersby. Of course, Selfridge's vision was of a store that would be a popular attraction all on its own, and with the right amenities he thought it could pull in a good share of the crowds around Marble Arch.

After returning home, Selfridge sat down to do some serious planning. It didn't take him long to decide that the idea was practical. He could afford to build and launch a store near Marble Arch, and keep it going until it began to make a profit. Retirement was over. Returning to London, he began looking for a suitable location. It didn't take him long to find one. He managed to buy a full block on the north side of Oxford Street, running from Orchard Street to Duke Street - a plot 180 yards long and 150 yards deep. Photos from the time show a row of mismatched four-story buildings in a variety of styles, with shops at street level and a mixture of office space and apartments above. There was no way the existing buildings could be converted into a department store, but that wasn't part of the plan anyway. Selfridge had rejuvenated one store and founded another, but both times he'd done so in an existing building. This time he had the chance to start with a blank slate and he intended to make the most of it. Within months of Selfridge buying it the entire block had been razed to the ground and a huge excavation was underway to make space for the foundations and basement levels of the new store.

In addition to its size the site of the new store had another major advantage. It was directly opposite one of the entrances to Bond Street Station, part of the London Underground network. Today two lines run through Bond Street Station, since the first section of the Jubilee Line was built in 1971. In 1906, there was only one line there but it was the Central Line, the busiest route on the whole network. That suited Selfridge's plans perfectly – every day thousands of people would pour out of that station entrance onto Oxford Street, and the first thing they saw would be his spectacular new store.

And it was certainly going to be spectacular. In total Selfridge was investing £400,000 in the new store. In 1906, one Pound Sterling was worth about $4.85, so the total sum was close to two million dollars. Adjusted into 2014 dollars, that's a billion dollar project, and the investment paid off. Selfridge would have liked to build the biggest department store in the country but that wasn't feasible; Harrods had opened their new building in 1905 and it was enormous; its sales floors had a total area of more than a million square feet. More than a century later it's still Europe's largest department store by a long way; the runner-up, Berlin's KaDeWe, comes in at a mere 650,000 square feet. Harrods could build such a huge structure because of their location but Selfridge was constrained by the street grid in central London. The largest he could manage was 540,000 square feet of retail space, still enough to be (both then and now) the second largest department store in the UK. That was an impressive achievement on its own, but to make it an even more attractive place to visit he carefully applied every one of the lessons he'd learned in Chicago.

For the actual design of the building Selfridge brought in an American architect, Daniel Burnham. It was an obvious choice; in addition to New York's famous Flatiron Building Burnham had designed the Marshall Field store, so he and Selfridge were already acquainted. Burnham had a solid understanding of how a department store should be built and that, combined with Selfridge's genius for retail, gave the pair all the skills they needed to come up with something special. What they had in mind was a building like nothing London had ever seen before.

The two building materials most associated with London are Portland stone, a high quality pale gray limestone, and the ubiquitous red brick. Between them these materials give the city center much of its character; most prominent pre-20th century buildings are constructed from one or both of them. To fit in with the surroundings, Burnham and Selfridge decided to stay with them, but they were looking for a radically different style. Because London doesn't face any earthquake hazard, large buildings of brick (with or without stone facing) or of stone blocks are very durable, but the characteristics of the materials put a limit on the way they can be designed; to give enough structural rigidity, the size of windows and other openings has to be kept relatively small. That can be seen from looking at Harrods. Although the massive building has hundreds of windows they're not very large, and most of the façade is stone. London's famously damp weather means that in pre-central heating days the natives didn't see this as a problem; thick stone or brick walls are a much better insulator than a pane of window glass. However, Selfridge wanted the store to be as bright and airy as he could manage and there was a way to do that. Again Burnham turned out to be the idea choice. He'd been able to build the Flatiron because New York had changed its building codes in 1892. Before then the law required that buildings had to use solid masonry for its fireproof properties. With the change he could now use steel frame construction, making the 22-story Flatiron possible. Selfridge also knew the benefits of steel framed buildings after his experiment at Harrose Hall, and was keen to use the same technology for the new store. That would allow much larger windows, because they were no longer limited by the width of a stone lintel. There was only one problem: London's building codes hadn't been updated.

Building regulations in the capital were set by London City Council, and the last major update had been in 1844. Earthquakes might not have been a problem in London but fire was, and after the city's incineration in 1666, planners were always conscious of the danger. Wooden buildings had almost vanished from the city after the Great Fire, and masonry – and, later, brick – were prized for their unwillingness to burn. Even if a brick building did burn out, the walls would help to contain the fire and prevent it spreading. Steel frame construction was new, and before the City Council would let Selfridge and Burnham build their store they would have to show that, in the event of a fire, it wouldn't collapse and spill burning debris into the surrounding blocks. Selfridge and Burnham started looking for a precedent, and they also found an engineer who could design the building's frame. Sven Bylander was a Swedish structural specialist who'd learned about steel as a draftsman in a shipyard then applied his knowledge to buildings in Germany and the USA.[xviii] Now he searched London for any sign of steel buildings – and he got lucky. At the time, the city was a major commercial port and the Docklands district, now a middle to high income residential area, was a maze of docks and warehouses. Many of the warehouses were brick, but some of the more recent ones were steel-framed. The owners had managed to persuade the City Council that this method had a lot of advantages – greater interior space being a major one – and was safe enough. If it could be used for something as notoriously flammable as a warehouse there was no reason to rule it out for a department store, so Bylander prepared some initial plans and made contact with the Metropolitan Buildings Office.

British Buildings Offices are famous for their slow-moving conservative approach to new innovations, but Bylander seems to have been luckier than most applicants. Perhaps the planners were eager to catch up with New York; in any case they were willing to consider the plans and soon Bylander was working with them to solve their remaining worries. They agreed on a deep foundation of brick piers, supporting a total of eight floors – three basement levels and five above ground. The structure would be built around a steel frame with the piers extending up around its perimeter; the steel would support the concrete floor slabs at each level. Externally the piers were to be clad in Portland stone; the spaces between them would hold cast iron window frames, allowing for a huge area of glazing. Decorative columns from the second to fourth floors were added to give the building a suitably dramatic appearance. The Buildings Office still had some worries about fire, so they ruled that no single space inside the building could be larger than 450,000 cubic feet.[xix] Bylander agreed, but he hoped this rule would be relaxed in the future (it was) so he made sure the necessary partitions would be easily removable. Again, the steel frame helped; the partitions met the required fire resistance standard but were kept as light as possible and were supported by the framework. They had no structural role in the building and could be removed without damaging its strength. The maximum size of internal doorway was also doubled, to allow 12 by 12-foot openings; this allowed daylight to penetrate into the center of each floor even with the partitions in place. In 1907, the Buildings Office approved the new design and construction began.

Yet again, the chosen construction method paid off. Selfridge wanted to get the store open as soon as possible, but putting up such a large building would take time. Harrods, built using more traditional methods, had taken eleven years to complete. Because the steel framework was built in prefabricated sections that were assembled on site, however, it was possible to build it in sections. The frontage of the store was split into "bays", each separated by a brick pier; the plan was for 20 bays in total, ten each side of the main entrance. To meet Selfridge's initial time scale, the first phase consisted of building nine bays at the Duke Street end of the store, complete with a temporary entrance. The resulting store was only a quarter the size of Harrods, but Burnham and Bylander managed to build it in a year and a half.

With the truncated building complete, it was time for Selfridge to take over. This was his chance to put all his ideas into effect with no constraints imposed by the location. One of those ideas was about space. Previous department stores had been divided into a series of distinct rooms, with Liberty being an extreme example. The new one turned that on its head. Each floor was still split up into departments but, except where the fire partitions made it necessary, that wouldn't be done by walls. Instead elaborate displays would mark the borders between one department and the next, with leaving sightlines as open as possible. Thanks to the big, permanently open doors in the partitions – Bylander pioneered the use of concertina shutters to close them when necessary – it was often possible to look from one end of a floor to another. This gave the store an open feeling, and left the prominent displays visible to tempt people into other departments. To aid this effect Selfridge even redesigned the internal furniture. Most store counters at the time were designed to be at mid-chest height; instead these, and as many other items as possible, would be kept to waist level.[xx] Again, this added to the feeling of spaciousness.

Selfridge's efforts didn't end at making the sales floors look good. There were nine elevators throughout the building to speed customers between floors, as well as eight staircases for the more nervous. Escalators were already in existence but weren't very popular; unlike the familiar modern design with its smoothly sliding metal steps, the early models were simply leather belts with wooden cleats to stop the passengers' feet from slipping. When Harrods installed one in 1898, they famously offered free smelling salts and cognac at the top to revive nervous riders.[xxi] That was a gimmick to make the store look daring and cutting-edge, but many people really did feel uncomfortable about using them so Selfridge stuck with the more acceptable elevators.

The in-store restaurants were also part of Selfridge's plan. Eating out in central London can get expensive quickly, and the middle-class shoppers Selfridge wanted to attract would be reluctant to visit the fast food shops of the time – jellied eel stands or pie shops, which were often filled with terrifyingly drunk laborers. An elegant but inexpensive restaurant in a central location had the potential to bring in a lot of diners, and if it brought them into the store so much the better. Several restaurants were located throughout the store, each catering to a different type of customer. A conservatory on the roof terrace housed an upscale formal restaurant, while others catered to families, fashionable young people or shoppers with limited time on their hands. A tearoom offered quality cakes, and small stands in the food hall gave shoppers a sample of the many delicacies on offer there.

Selfridge's grand concept even took account of London's place as the center of a huge empire and its importance for international trade. Although he expected most of his customers to be Londoners or visitors from elsewhere in Britain, he went out of his way to make overseas visitors feel welcome. There were special rooms for American, French, German and "Colonial" guests, with décor and music chosen to make them feel at home. A library gave the studious a place to relax. For everyone else there was a "silence room" which offered comfortable chairs, double glazing and soft ambient lights.[xxii] Every feature was carefully devised to bring people into the store and persuade them to stay as long as possible.

By early 1909, the store was finished and ready for the public. Staff was recruited – a total of 1,400 employees were taken on.[xxiii] All of them had to be trained in Harry's new way of doing things. Those who would be working on the sales floors were taught the correct way to interact with customers – helpful, but not pushy. If a customer looked around for assistance there should be someone close by, but nobody would be badgered by hard-selling staff. Selfridge had his own reasons for disliking this approach. Not long after he'd first come to London he'd been browsing in a store when a floorwalker approached him. "Is Sir intending to buy something?" the man asked in an impeccable British accent. Selfridge replied, "No, I'm just looking." Instantly the good manners vanished – "Then 'op it, mate."[xxiv] That wasn't how he wanted his own customers to be treated, so floorwalkers weren't part of his staff requirements.

Employees were also taught how to demonstrate products to customers. Electrical appliances were starting to become more common at the time and the store would carry a wide range of them, and Selfridge believed that showing them in action was a good way to encourage sales.

In the early weeks of 1909, the London newspapers were flooded with adverts for the new store. For the time the publicity campaign was huge and elaborate, offering tantalizing hints about the store's luxury and the range of goods available inside. By early March, London was buzzing with excitement. When Selfridge's opened on March 15, 1909, it was an elaborately choreographed spectacle. As the minutes ticked away toward the announced opening time crowds formed in the street outside. The doors were closed; silk curtains covered every one of the big plate glass windows. Then, at precisely 9:00am, a bugler stepped out onto the balcony above the entrance and blew a fanfare. Simultaneously, the doors swung open and every one of the curtains rose together, uncovering displays of fashionable clothing modeled by mannequins in lifelike poses. By the end of the day 90,000 people had been counted entering the store.[xxv] Selfridge's had been an instant success.[xxvi]

Chapter 5: The Golden Years

The five years after the new store opened were probably the high point of Harry Selfridge's life. He had achieved yet another massive business success, creating a revolutionary new retail outlet in the world's most important city. He had his wife and four children. The public admired him and his fellow businessmen held him in immense respect. The plans were ready for the expansion of the store to its full planned size and the money he would need to carry out the work was accumulating rapidly. He managed to persuade the General Post Office, who ran Britain's telephone network at the time, to give the store the telephone number 1. Anyone who wanted to be put through to Selfridge's simply had to call the operator and ask for Garrard, which in the days before direct dial made it much easier to get through. Flushed with success, Harry even went as far as to suggest cutting a tunnel from the store's basement level to Bond Street Station, which he proposed should be renamed Selfridge's Station. That was a step too far even for him – the idea was shot down by combined public and official opposition. The attempt didn't dent the store's popularity, though.

With the store open, Harry had been joined in England by Rose and their children. As a family residence, he bought Lansdowne House, a large mansion on Berkeley Square. It was a spectacular house, designed by the famous architect Robert Adam, and had belonged to three former British prime ministers. Rose loved the house and enthusiastically joined in with London society, giving harp performances – she was an excellent harpist – and hosting parties that became hugely popular.

What was less popular, certainly with Rose, was Harry's womanizing. His sudden prominence in London society, and his huge wealth, attracted a stream of curious women and he found it very hard to resist them. He had a less than discreet affair with Syrie Wellcome, the estranged wife of an American pharmaceuticals millionaire. His name was linked with Russian ballerina Anna Pavlova and a string of other prominent society women. Rose never said a word, probably in the interests of domestic harmony, but often Selfridge's latest real or assumed conquest was the talk of the town.

There were other low points as well. In 1911, the family was on holiday in the Lake District, in the north of England. It's one of the most beautiful parts of the country but the roads are often steep and winding, weaving a dangerous path through the valleys carved out by the last Ice Age. Descending one hill toward the resort town of Ambleside on Lake Windermere, their car's brakes failed and the car raced downhill out of control. Finally it came off the road and slammed into the side of a house, throwing its occupants onto the ground. Harry suffered serious cuts and a concussion that left him unconscious for almost a day. Rose suffered two broken bones in one arm, and Harry's mother Lois and daughter Rosalie Junior were both badly bruised. The accident dampened Rose's enthusiasm for life in England, and she began to make more frequent trips back to Chicago to visit her family. Soon, a bigger tragedy would make even that dangerous.

The First World War broke out on July 28, 1914, after a period of tension between the great European powers. Within a year it would expand out of control to become the largest conflict the world had yet seen, but at first, its impact on London was limited. Between Britain's huge Royal Navy and the powerful armies of France and Russia it was expected that Germany and her allies would be defeated within months, and the country was swept by a wave of patriotic fervor. In most respects, life went on as normal, though. The British Army was an all-volunteer force and relatively small, so it didn't disrupt society when a large part of it was sent to France. Most people in London went right on with their lives and business at Selfridge's continued to boom. When the Army began recruiting on a large scale later that year it was another boost for many retailers. While soldiers were issued everything they would need, officers were expected to buy several items themselves, such as a handgun and binoculars, and there were many other optional pieces of equipment they could purchase. For example, the Burberry trench coat was a popular, and authorized, replacement for the heavy woolen greatcoat the Army provided. Selfridge's was the ideal place to stock up on high quality items before boarding a train to the Channel ports. By late 1915 thousands of men were dying every day in the trenches of the Western Front, but

Selfridge's continued to prosper.

In 1916 the war started to extend its tentacles further afield. Germany had built a fleet of Zeppelin airships and they could carry bombs. Their payload was neither very large nor very accurate, and in fact in the early years of the war the Kaiser had forbidden any raids on London, but by the end of 1914, the enormous craft were roaming over the cities of Poland, Greece and Belgium at night dropping bombs. Nobody could say how long London's apparent immunity would last, and Harry decided to look for a place away from the huge target of the city.[xxvii] He found Highcliffe Castle, a Dorset mansion about 80 miles southwest of London. Despite its medieval name and appearance, Highcliffe was actually a Georgian villa, built between 1831 and 1835, but large amounts of salvaged medieval stonework from two old Norman churches had been used in its construction. It was a huge home with extensive grounds including elaborate formal gardens, and had earned some publicity in 1907 when Kaiser Wilhelm II – now the figurehead of Britain's enemies, but formerly a friendly foreign relative of Queen Victoria – had spent three weeks there recovering from an illness. Two stained glass windows presented by the German leader had been installed in the house to mark the event. The recipient of these gifts, Edward Montagu-Stuart-Wortley, was an officer in the British Army and was now a Major General serving in France. He didn't particularly need Highcliffe at the time, and owned other homes in any case, so when Selfridge offered to lease it from him he was happy to accept. In fact, Selfridge treated the house as if he'd bought it, having substantial improvements carried out. A new kitchen, modern bathrooms and a central heating system were some of the more notable changes he made.[xxviii]

Meanwhile, Rose was getting involved in the war effort. As an American citizen neither Britain nor her own government would let her get directly involved in war work, but the Red Cross had no such scruples and were busily recruiting volunteers. The couple's two older daughters, Rosalie and Violette, joined the Red Cross and worked at Christchurch Hospital. Rose also signed up but her skills took her in a different direction. Unlike today, most people in 1916 couldn't drive, and there was a desperate shortage of ambulance drivers. Many American men signed up to help transport the wounded from the front line back to field hospitals in France; to free up more men for this vital role women who could drive were recruited to work in England. Rose could drive, so she found herself in a Red Cross uniform carrying wounded men from the Channel ports to hospitals around southern England.

Meanwhile Harry, still busy running the store, had even grander plans for the family. Highcliffe was only a lease, but he had decided to acquire a permanent home on the picturesque Dorset coast and he started making enquiries about buying Hengistbury Head, a mile-long promontory two miles west of Highcliffe. The Head and the sandbar that ran from its end enclosed a natural harbor, and Selfridge planned to build himself a grand castle-style home there. However, these plans were interrupted in 1917 by a new development in the war.

Since fighting broke out in 1914, US President Woodrow Wilson had been sticking to a policy of non-interference in European affairs. Public opinion was split at first, with one segment of the population supporting Britain while Americans of German, Swedish and Irish descent, along with a majority of women and religious leaders, favoring neutrality or even an alliance with Germany. As the war went on and reports of German atrocities against Belgian civilians (most of which later proved to be false) started to filter through opinion began to swing more solidly toward the British side, especially after the famous transatlantic liner RMS *Lusitania* was sunk by a German U-Boat in 1915. Wilson officially maintained neutrality but began making large loans available to Britain and France to help them finance their war efforts. Finally, in early 1917, two events came together in a perfect storm of diplomatic outrage. First, Germany announced that unrestricted submarine warfare against ships sailing to Britain – which had been suspended after the *Lusitania* sinking – would be resumed. As American ships were still trading freely with the British, that made it almost inevitable that some would be sunk. Secondly, British Naval Intelligence intercepted and decoded a telegram from Germany to their embassy in Mexico City. This ultra-secret message told the ambassador to offer the Mexicans an alliance if the USA entered the war on the British side; the effect would have been to expand the war to North America and open a new front along the US-Mexican border. That would have been the end of the matter, if it wasn't for the British. Realizing the potential of their intercept they immediately handed it to the US embassy in London. At first the ambassador rejected it as a provocation but the British were ready for that, and the Germans had been too clever for their own good. They had actually used US diplomatic channels to send the telegram, persuading the Berlin embassy to accept a coded signal, so the USA had the encrypted text. Now the British simply handed over the cipher key and invited the Americans to read it for themselves. Just to be on the safe side they publicly announced the discovery, although to conceal their code-breaking success they claimed to have broken an older, easier code used by the Mexican telegraph office.

The American public was understandably outraged at the "Zimmermann Telegram" and its revelations of hostile plotting. Pro-German agitators in the USA tried to dismiss it as a British plot, but then the Germans shot themselves spectacularly in the foot. Foreign secretary Arthur Zimmermann, the author of the telegram, held a press conference in Berlin on March 3 at which he admitted it was authentic, but justified himself by saying the alliance would only have gone into effect if the USA joined the war. The timing, from his point of view, was not good. The U-Boats had resumed unrestricted attacks on February 1 and two American ships had already gone to the bottom of the Atlantic. President Wilson proposed using US Navy seamen and guns to defend merchant shipping, a move that was opposed by pacifists in the Senate. That refusal just inflamed public opinion even more and on April 6 a joint session of Congress voted to declare war on Germany. The first units of the US Navy and US Marines were on their way to Europe within weeks.

With their nation now fighting on the Allied side, the Selfridges were more connected to the war than they had been before. Its epic tragedy was soon brought home to them in a dramatic way, though. The British and French (and their German opponents) had been fighting a brutal war in the trenches for three years. They'd learned how the power of machine guns and modern artillery paralyzed movement, and that frontal attacks were simply suicidal. The newly arriving Americans hadn't learned these lessons and thought their new allies were simply timid. Fearing disaster, the British and French commanders recommended that US battalions be distributed among existing Allied divisions as reinforcements, but General John J. Pershing was adamant: his men would fight as US divisions and they would follow US doctrine. That called for frontal assaults, and the result was appalling. The Germans were awed by the bravery of the fresh US troops, but that didn't stop them from mowing them down by the thousand as they charged straight at dug-in German machine guns. It didn't take long before Pershing, who was a talented and flexible officer, realized that the British and French had been right; US doctrine was quickly changed to mirror that of the British. By that time, thousands of American soldiers were dead, however, and many more had been seriously wounded and evacuated to England.

By this time the Selfridges had been in England for eleven years and were well settled there, but they still thought of themselves as Americans. Now hospitals across the country were filled with young men from their homeland. Some were out of the war and would be returning to the USA; others, less seriously wounded, would be rejoining their units. All of them needed someplace they could rest and recover from their injuries, and the military hospitals that were springing up were stretched to the limit. Rose, who'd always been an energetic woman with a great deal of personal initiative, wanted to help them if she could. Of course, she could always continue her ambulance work, but she felt there was more that could be done. Finally, she hit on the idea of creating a rest camp where wounded men could convalesce. The advantage of living in a huge country house was that there was plenty of space for a project like that, and of course they had the money to arrange it. Highcliffe's cricket pavilion was converted into an administration office for the camp, quarters were built for a US Army NCO who would be in charge of discipline and a dozen huts were built to house wounded soldiers. A recreation room offered a range of ways to pass the time: books and games, writing materials for letters home, maps for those who wanted to track the progress of the war and a gramophone with a small library of vinyl disks.[xxix] The facility was grandly named "The Mrs. Gordon Selfridge Convalescent Camp For American Soldiers", and the first wounded men arrived in late 1917. By the end of the war, hundreds of soldiers had passed through it, either to gain the strength needed for the long voyage home through U-Boat infested waters, or as a blessed pause before being thrown back into the carnage of the Western Front. The whole project was organized with Rose's characteristic energy and enthusiasm.

Sadly, though, the convalescent camp was to be Rose's last project. By early 1918 the long stalemate in France was slowly beginning to break down and an Allied victory was at last in sight. On the horizon, however, was an even greater outbreak of death and suffering that over the next two years would come to overshadow the war itself.

Chapter 6: Tragedy

Influenza, more commonly known by the deceptively harmless name "the flu," has been with us for a very long time. The first person to describe its symptoms was the Greek father of medicine, Hippocrates, writing about 2,400 years ago. It seems to have originated in Europe and sailors carried it with them throughout the great age of exploration. In 1493, shortly after Christopher Columbus arrived in the New World, most of the population of the Antilles was killed by a disease that sounds suspiciously like flu. Major outbreaks continued for centuries, sometimes killing thousands of people. It was an age of plagues, though, and when cholera or typhus could decimate a city's population in a matter of weeks – and where fond memories of the Black Death lingered – flu didn't seem too bad. People had a healthy respect for it, but they thought they knew what the disease was capable of. They were horribly mistaken.

Influenza is normally an unpleasant disease that can put an adult in bed for a week of absolute misery and might kill small children, the elderly or those with respiratory problems. In January 1918, a different strain of the virus began to spread. It had started late the year before in Étaples, in northern France; modern epidemiologists believe a strain of avian flu mutated to infect pigs kept near the front line for army rations, then mutated again and made the jump to humans in a huge transit camp near the town. There was also a field hospital there and the virus quickly reached it, either through direct transmission, or when men who'd passed through the camp reached the front, became seriously ill and were evacuated back to the hospital. From Étaples the disease was brought back to England in the bodies of sick soldiers; horrifyingly, the medical evacuation system, the most efficient ever devised up to that time, seems to have unwittingly acted as a highway network for the mutant strain of H1N1 flu. It reached Kansas by the end of January 1918, only days after it was first reported in England. By March, it was in New York. This first wave of infection resembled a more virulent form of normal flu; the young, old and weak were most at risk. A second wave erupted in August that turned the rules on their head; over the summer the virus had evolved yet again, and now it triggered its victims' immune systems into attacking their own bodies. This wave was far deadlier and hit healthy younger adults the hardest, but the first wave was quite lethal enough. By the time the second mutation began its swathe of destruction, up to 25 million people were already dead and, in early May, the disease had reached Highcliffe.

Rose Selfridge was 57 years old and in good health. Normally she would have shrugged off an attack of flu after a few days in bed drinking lemon tea and chicken soup, but this flu wasn't normal. Even the less terrifying first wave was a killer and Rose was just old enough to be in real danger. Sometime in the first week of May, the infection was brought into the convalescent camp, probably by a sick soldier or an ambulance driver, and Rose was exposed to it. The virus laid her low with terrifying speed, and before her body even had a chance to fight it off her weakened immune system was overwhelmed by a secondary infection: pneumonia. Before the introduction of antibiotics, pneumonia was a very serious condition with few treatment options available, and although there were army medical staff nearby, Rose's condition went downhill rapidly. She died on May 12, 1918, less than a week after first feeling ill.

Rose's body lay in state in the great hall of Highcliffe Castle, covered by a silk sheet on which Selfridge's employees had embroidered 3,000 red roses.[xxx] Her funeral service was held on May 16 in St. Mark's Church, Highcliffe, and she was buried in the cemetery there in a shaded plot under a row of ancient trees. Selfridge erected an elaborate headstone for her; a relief carved on it depicted an angel holding a plaque with her name.

With Rose gone, Violetta took over her work at the convalescent camp and Harry threw himself back into running the store. Within months of her death, Rosalie Jr. married Serge de Bolotoff, a Russian aristocrat. The family that had come to England in 1909 was broken and scattering, and Selfridge's own life started to tip slowly into a long decline. He had a long way to fall, though, and a few triumphs still to come.

Chapter 7: After The War

In his spare moments since opening the London store, Harry Selfridge had been working on a book. When he could motivate himself again after Rose's death, he published it. It was called *The Romance Of Commerce* and it was a history of retailing through the ages. He also moved forward with his plans for Hengistbury Head, purchasing the land in 1919. His plan was to build an enormous castle there, with 250 bedrooms, a private theater and a surrounding wall four miles long. For the first time, though, he was making a plan that he would never carry through. The work of designing the castle progressed in fits and starts but building work never began.

Tragedy struck again in 1924 when his mother Lois, his constant companion for his entire life, died suddenly. She was buried beside Rose in the Highcliffe churchyard, and once again he set about going on with his life. Enough time had passed since Rose's death for him to re-enter the social scene and he embarked on a new series of relationships. Among the women he was linked to over the next few years were the Dolly Sisters, identical twins who had achieved some fame as dancers and actresses. A string of other showgirls followed, and he lavished money and gifts on all of them. He was also indulging his love of gambling, but unfortunately, his enthusiasm outpaced his luck and he lost a steady stream of money. He lost £5,000 at casinos in 1921, when the average wage in Britain was around £500 a year.[xxxi] It didn't help that the Dolly Sisters were also gambling addicts; the three of them would visit casinos and racetracks together, and they helped him gamble away up to £5 million. None of it mattered much, though; the store was as popular as ever, and in fact was expanding. In 1927, the second half of the building opened, doubling the retail area and adding the spectacular grand entrance on Oxford Street. As the building code was modernized, many of the internal partitions were torn down, making the sales floors even more spacious than before. Twenty years of advances in building technology meant the new areas were even more revolutionary than the original section, and the business went from strength to strength. Selfridge's personal fortune was slowly declining as money flowed out on horses and actresses, but as long as he was at the head of such a successful business, he was as financially secure as anyone could be.

Then, in 1929, it all went wrong. The stock market in the USA had been climbing steeply for several years; millions of people were getting wealthy as share prices continued on a seemingly endless upward trajectory. Prices can't rise forever, though. At some point they have to return to equilibrium, and in early September the first jitters hit the New York exchanges. After a few days, prices seemed to rally and business went on as before, but on October 29 – now known as Black Tuesday – the bottom fell out of the market. With the loss of investments, industrial production started to plummet; by 1932, output had fallen by 46 per cent in the USA, and 23 per cent in Britain – and unemployment rocketed. Suddenly people were spending less, threatening Selfridge's revenue stream, and Harry himself found that the volume of his investments had been slashed. Of course, he still wasn't poor, but for the first time in his life he was forced to retreat. He had given up the lease on Highcliffe in 1922, but now he had to sell Lansdowne House and move into a more modest home. Hengistbury Head was sold in 1930, finally ending his dreams of building a castle.

The Great Depression dragged on, with the low point coming in 1932. By then 3.5 million people in Britain were unemployed and profits in the retail sector, especially in the luxury end, were greatly reduced. Selfridge's was still making a profit but the board of directors were in a cautious mood, and they were rapidly losing patience with Harry's spendthrift ways. As the 1930s went on the economy slowly began to recover but Harry's personal fortune didn't. He was still spending money too fast, and was starting to run up considerable debts. His relations with the board grew increasingly heated as they repeatedly urged him to be more prudent. Their demands grew stronger after the Second World War began in September 1939, until finally they could take no more. Harry's debts had reached a quarter of a million pounds and the board, fearing that they would end up being liable for them, took the extraordinary step of forcing out the company's founder.[xxxii]

For Harry Selfridge, this was the end of the line as a businessman. He was 83 years old and deeply in debt. The board had awarded him a reasonable pension, but it was nowhere near enough to continue with the lifestyle he'd become accustomed to. From a multimillionaire with two luxury homes he was now reduced to a pensioner living in a rented apartment in Putney, a lower middle class area in southwest London. He shared the flat with his oldest daughter Rosalie but, for the first time in his life, his days were empty.

Cut loose from the store he'd founded and too old to contemplate starting again, Selfridge entered a steady decline. His hearing began to fail and his mind often wandered. He and Rosalie managed to get by on his pension, as he had all the clothes and other possessions he would ever need, but there was little left over for luxuries. Sometimes when he could spare a few pence, he would catch a bus to Oxford Street and gaze at the magnificent building he had created. Almost certainly he let his thoughts drift back to the heady days when his revolutionary new store had taken London's shoppers by storm. The store went on, of course, but he was no longer part of it. When General Eisenhower took over part of the basement as his headquarters, attracted by its bombproof concrete floors and the secure telex lines Harry had had installed, he knew nothing about it. The days when he could walk boldly in the great entrance and up to the chairman's office were long gone. Once, as he gazed sadly at his legacy, the police mistook him for a vagrant and arrested him.

Harry Gordon Selfridge died in his sleep on the night of May 8, 1947. He was 91 years old. His funeral was arranged on a low budget and his grave, in the Highcliffe churchyard close to his wife and mother, is marked only by a plain headstone paid for by his daughter Rosalie:

IN LOVING MEMORY

HARRY GORDON SELFRIDGE

1857-1947

Conclusion

Harry Selfridge's own life ended on a depressing note, with his wealth gone and his career brutally ended by the business he'd created. The Selfridge's brand lives on, though. There are now four stores in total, with two in Manchester and one in Birmingham, and the company has created several sub-brands to attract new types of customers. The flagship of the company, now owned by Canadian billionaire Galen Weston, is still the huge store on Oxford Street. On the outside, its imposing neoclassical façade seems timeless; inside, it's been remodeled time after time, keeping it up to date with the latest developments in marketing and customer service.

What would Harry Selfridge have thought of what his store has become? It's almost certain he would have been delighted. His retail career was marked by his willingness to innovate, to take risks and to go about things in a completely new way. Selfridge's, Oxford Street remains the store he created *because* it changes with the times; if it kept on doing things in the same old way, it wouldn't be the business he founded.

Like all of us, Selfridge had character flaws. His womanizing and love of an expensive lifestyle were, ultimately, self-destructive. He made up for it by a genuine devotion to his family and an enthusiastic compulsion to give his customers an experience they'd never had before. He succeeded, too. We may take the shopping experience for granted, but we can only do that because Harry Selfridge created it for us.

[i] Fond du Lac County Local History Web, *D.P. Mapes' Account of Early Ripon, 1870*
  http://www.wlhn.org/fond_du_lac/towns/ripon_mapes.htm
[ii] Wisconsin Historical Society, *The origin of the Republican Party*

http://content.wisconsinhistory.org/cdm/compoundobject/collection/tp/id/46379/show/46363
[iii] Selfridges.com, *Images*
  http://images.selfridges.com/is/image/selfridges/herit-timeline-01?scl=1
[iv] Woodhead, Lindy (2013), *Shopping, Seduction & Mr Selfridge*
[v] Milwaukee Journal, Sep 7, 1932, *The Yankee Who Taught Britishers That "The Customer Is Always Right"*
http://www.wisconsinhistory.org/wlhba/articleView.asp?pg=1&orderby=&id=11176&pn=1&key=selfridge&cy=
[vi] Milwaukee Journal, Sep 7, 1932, *The Yankee Who Taught Britishers That "The Customer Is Always Right"*
http://www.wisconsinhistory.org/wlhba/articleView.asp?pg=1&orderby=&id=11176&pn=1&key=selfridge&cy=
[vii] Justia, *Laidlaw v. Organ – 15 U.S. 178 (1817)*
  http://supreme.justia.com/cases/federal/us/15/178/case.html
[viii] Not Always Right, *Funny & Stupid Customer Stories*
  http://notalwaysright.com/
[ix] US Census Bureau, *Facts: The Holiday Season*
  http://www.census.gov/Press-Release/www/releases/archives/facts_for_features_special_editions/005870.html
[x] Brave New Talent, *Selfridges*
  http://www.bravenewtalent.com/selfridges
[xi] Comley, W.J. and Eggville, W.D. (1875), *Ohio: The Future Great State*

http://archive.org/stream/ohiofuturegreats00coml#page/n3/mode/2up

[xii] Buckingham, J. (1892), *The Ancestors of Ebenezer Buckingham*

http://archive.org/stream/ancestorsofebene00buck#page/n9/mode/2up

[xiii] Woodhead, Lindy (2013), *Shopping, Seduction & Mr Selfridge*

[xiv] Glessner House Museum Blog, *Harry Gordon Selfridge - The Chicago Years*
http://glessnerhouse.blogspot.de/2013/04/harry-gordon-selfridge-chicago-years.html

[xv] Lake Geneva News, Jan 8, 2004, *The Chatterbox*
http://www.lakegenevanews.net/Articles-i-2004-01-08-67545.112112_The_Chatterbox.html

[xvi] *Largest US cities by population – 1900*
http://www.biggestuscities.com/ny/1900

[xvii] Culture24, July 14, 2000, *Shopping in London, Roman Style*
http://www.culture24.org.uk/history-and-heritage/time/roman/20000714-07

[xviii] The Structural Engineer, 1943, *Obituary: Mr S. Bylander*
http://www.istructe.org/journal/volumes/volume-21-(published-in-1943)/issues/issue-11/articles/obituary-mr-s-bylander

[xix] Goodman, David C. (1999), *The European Cities And Technology Reader: Industrial to Post-Industrial City*

[xx] Goodman, David C. (1999), The European Cities And Technology Reader: Industrial to Post-Industrial City

[xxi] The Draper's Record, November 19, 1898, *The First Moving Staircase In England*

[xxii] The Royal Purveyors, *Selfridges: pioneers of Oxford Street*
http://www.theroyalpurveyors.com/fashion/selfridges/

[xxiii] Goodman, David C. (1999), *The European Cities And Technology Reader: Industrial to Post-Industrial City*

[xxiv] Woodhead, Lindy (2013), *Shopping, Seduction & Mr Selfridge*

[xxv] Selfridge's, Oxford Street celebrates 100 years, *Media update*
http://www.z-pr.com/pdf/09-03-11_selfridges.pdf

[xxvi] Spy Hollywood, *The Real Mrs Selfridge vs. The TV Mrs Selfridge*
http://spyhollywood.com/the-real-mrs-selfridge-verses-the-tv-mrs-selfridge/

[xxvii] The Bournemouth Echo, February 8, 2014, *Mr Selfridge's Castle*
http://m.bournemouthecho.co.uk/news/10991379.Mr_Selfridge_s_Castle__When_Harry_Selfridge_came_to_Highcliffe_Castle/

[xxviii] Woodhead, Lindy (2013), *Shopping, Seduction & Mr Selfridge*

[xxix] Spy Hollywood, *The Real Mrs Selfridge vs. The TV Mrs Selfridge*
http://spyhollywood.com/the-real-mrs-selfridge-verses-the-tv-mrs-selfridge/

[xxx] The Bournemouth Echo, February 8, 2014, *Mr Selfridge's Castle*
http://m.bournemouthecho.co.uk/news/10991379.Mr_Selfridge_s_Castle__When_Harry_Selfridge_came_to_Highcliffe_Castle/

[xxxi] Tweedland, *Who Was The True Harry Gordon Selfridge?*
http://tweedlandthegentlemansclub.blogspot.de/2014/03/who-was-true-harry-selfridge.html

[xxxii] The Bournemouth Echo, February 8, 2014, *Mr Selfridge's Castle*
http://m.bournemouthecho.co.uk/news/10991379.Mr_Selfridge_s_Castle__When_Harry_Selfridge_came_to_Highcliffe_Castle/

CPSIA information can be obtained at www.ICGtesting.com
Printed in the USA
LVOW11s1545290715

448106LV00024B/1451/P

W9-CZB-561

ALREADY PUBLISHED

WILHELM REICH / Charles Rycroft
MOHANDAS GANDHI / George Woodcock
BERTRAND RUSSELL / A. J. Ayer
NORMAN MAILER / Richard Poirier
V. I. LENIN / Robert Conquest
EINSTEIN / Jeremy Bernstein
C. G. JUNG / Anthony Storr
D. H. LAWRENCE / Frank Kermode
KARL POPPER / Bryan Magee
SAMUEL BECKETT / A. Alvarez
R. D. LAING / Edgar Z. Friedenberg
MARCEL PROUST / Roger Shattuck

MODERN MASTERS

EDITED BY frank kermode

max
weber

donald g. macrae

THE VIKING PRESS | NEW YORK

To Mairi and Helen with love

PREFACE

In this little book I have approached Max Weber by indirection. To the center of a maze there is no other path, and I believe that Weber indeed presents us with a maze. One of the disappointments about real mazes is that at their hearts there is often nothing. I do not, however, think this true of Weber, though there is in my view less than has often been believed to lie hidden there. But the maze and its contents have certainly been sufficient to make of Weber one of the master figures of the social imagination in this century.

In so short a treatment I have tried to avoid both too much apparatus of learning and, whenever possible, a German vocabulary, despite the fact that Weber's use of language is peculiarly difficult in all but two or three of his published works—and these exceptions were formal lectures. As a consequence, I have deliberately employed metaphor in my exposition, while trying not to do violence to Weber's thought. I hope the result may inform the curious about Weber as social scientist and even help some students by giving them a road map to a mind peculiarly inseparable from the problems of a particular life in a highly specific cultural situation. But I am well aware that about so various a scholar no finality can be attained.

My wife, for reasons I understand, has suggested that I should dedicate this book to the memory of J. N. Hummel. I have, however, chosen not to do so.

Donald G. MacRae

CONTENTS

BIOGRAPHICAL NOTE

1864	Max Weber born at Erfurt, Thuringia, on April 21.
1869	Moves with his family to Berlin.
1879	Confirmed as church member.
1882	Student of economics, philosophy, and Roman law at Heidelberg University.
1883	Military service.
1884–1885	Student at Berlin.
1885–1886	Student at Göttingen.
1889	Completes thesis on medieval trading companies.
1891	Qualifies as university teacher with thesis on Roman agrarian and legal history.
1892	Teaches law in Berlin; marries Marianne Schnitzer.
1894	Professor of political economy at Freiburg.
1897	Professor of economics at Heidelberg. "Nervous breakdown."

1899–1904	Travels in Europe and North America.
1903	Made "Honorarprofessor"—i.e., put in semiretirement—at Heidelberg.
1904–1905	Publication of both parts of *The Protestant Ethic*.
1914–1918	Serves in hospital administration.
1918	Professor of sociology at Vienna.
1919	Professor of sociology at Munich.
1920	Dies on June 14.

MAX WEBER

The Reputation

●

i

The German sociologist Max Weber died at about five o'clock on the afternoon of June 14, 1920. The day had been wet and when Weber's student Karl Loewenstein visited the Weber home on the Seestrasse in Munich, he found the sick man alone. For a few minutes Loewenstein stayed by the bed, watching the last struggles of his teacher. Then he left. Weber's wife Marianne was elsewhere in the house, resting. Shortly after Loewenstein's departure Weber died, unattended and solitary. He was fifty-six years of age and he had occupied his professorial chair in Munich for only a few months. Had he lived, he intended to spend his next term at the university lecturing on socialism.

His death was a late consequence of the influenza pandemic which, starting in 1918, killed, it is believed, more people than died as casualties of the 1914–1918 war. By 1920 the disease had indeed become less virulent, but throughout Europe a population still weakened by privation, food rationing, and the effects of blockade remained vulnerable. Weber's case was not untypical. The influenza he had contracted in the early summer turned to pneumonia, and pneumonia —before the advances of chemotherapy in the 1930s— was usually fatal. Scholars, particularly original scholars in new and developing subjects, often ripen late. It has often been assumed that when Weber died he was on the threshold of a synthesis of the studies of his lifetime, but of this there can only be conjecture, not proof. Since his death his reputation has grown steadily, and his name is certainly far more widely known today than ever in his lifetime. What is the basis of this posthumous fame? At the level of popular repute I suggest that four factors are involved.

The first of these is very vulgar. In the 1960s it was a fashion among journalists and others to ascribe the quality of "charisma" to any public, dominant, and attractive person in the worlds of politics, entertainment, and the arts. Thus John F. Kennedy, Kwame Nkrumah, and the Beatles were all said to be "charismatic personalities." A kind of circular argument was employed either quite overtly or in a concealed form which ran: "X is an attractive figure in the public eye; therefore X has charisma; what makes X publicly attractive is his charisma. Charisma is at once proof, evidence, and cause of certain kinds of public success." Of course this quality was not ascribed to all public men equally, or at all. Kennedy—and, by extension, his family—were very charismatic; Khrushchev much less so. By the 1970s charisma was no longer a vogue-word. It was not claimed that Nixon, Heath, or Pompidou had charisma. We owe this usage of "charisma" largely to Weber. Whether it involves a distortion of what he had to say we shall see.

What, however, should be remembered is that Weber got the word from theology: to have charisma is to have divine grace, the grace of God, something, as Saint Thomas Aquinas said, "supernatural bestowed on man by God." Charisma then is not part of the natural order, not part of the material world, nor the world of society. It comes from without. What it is doing in the writings of a sociologist, concerned to understand so far as may be, by the ordinary means and concepts of science and scholarship, how people get along—or fail to get along —together is a good question.

The second factor contributing to Weber's place as an object of general awareness is to be found, at a slightly more rarefied level, in a metaphysical entity called "the Protestant ethic." I am not, of course, saying here that this concept is at all metaphysical in the actual writings of Weber, but simply that it operates metaphysically in a good deal of modern thought. Thus it is not uncommon to find the rapid growth rate of the economies of Japan, Singapore, and Hong Kong ascribed to the Protestant ethic—which in lands that have hardly known Christianity, far less Protestantism, is surprising. (In a rather more sophisticated form, the successes of these fortunate eastern isles is ascribed to "a functional equivalent for the Protestant ethic." I am not sure that this is much better.) Again, I know a textbook of history, widely used in British schools, in which the industrial revolution of the eighteenth century is explained by reference to the Protestant ethic of parsimony and dili-gence whereby both capital was accumulated and tech-nological discovery induced. This is surely as metaphysi-cal as the explanation offered in Molière's play *Le Malade imaginaire* that the somnolence resulting from opium is caused by the dormative principle in poppies. To these matters also we return later.

A third factor is the impact made on those who fre-quent libraries by the grim bulk of Weber's writings, writings which are composed in a style found difficult even by native German speakers and translated very often into either an English more obscure than the orig-inal, or into that extraordinary kind of French in which German nouns are borrowed—*le historischer Kausalzu-sammenhang*, for example. From these ranked volumes there emerges an atmosphere of prestige and oppression typical of much German nineteenth-century scholar-ship. The achievement of the German mind in the world of learning is a genuine one, but it is also very forbidding. Weber is part of it. His books are, particu-larly if they are not read, redolent of obscurity, knowl-edge, and a promise of revelation. As a result Weber is seen as a kind of Magus.

And there is an additional quality to these books which is at once mysterious and tantalizing. Very largely they consist of materials put together after his death. Weber was a man of enormous scholarly ambi-tion, sporadic and volcanic energy, and wide learning. As a result, a great deal that he intended to complete, fill out, or refine was left in a kind of chaos of articles, treatises, schema, lecture notes transcribed by students, and so on. This is not said in criticism, for no man in our century expects to die at fifty-six and no man should be condemned merely for attempting in the intellectual sphere more than he can actually accomplish. But the result is infuriating: eloquence, close reasoning, aridity, distinction for the sake of distinction, learning, and superficiality go together in his work. To consult Weber, therefore, is often somewhat like divination, like using a tarot pack or the I Ching. This does not necessarily harm a reputation and, given genuine eminence—and sometimes not even that—a reputation with this component is likely to give rise to another source of fame in the form of a learned industry of exposition, criticism, disputation, and interpretation. Internationally there is today a flourishing Weber industry. I am afraid this little book is another contribution to it.

But the fourth factor behind Weber's popular reputation is the most important. If the outlook of the nineteenth and early twentieth centuries was essentially dominated by historical attitudes and methods, so that Darwinism is a historical biology and Freudianism a historical psychology, the late twentieth century is an age of sociology. In sociology Weber is canonized. He is an accredited "founding father" of the discipline. He is an object not of skepticism or utility, but of piety. Even his critics like Herbert Marcuse are often under his spell. To many sociologists and most of the lay public he is the sociologist par excellence. It is very hard to think of a parallel case: a Marshall or a Keynes in economics, a Malinowski or a Radcliffe-Brown in anthropology, a Planck or an Einstein in physics are, of course, great historical names in their subjects. A student, a researcher, or a practitioner may gain refreshment, insight, and knowledge from returning to them; but their work has been winnowed and absorbed into their disciplines. Weber, on the other hand, is seen as more than this sort of figure. I called him a Magus: he is that, a living presence to professional sociologists as well as to the sociological laity, and a living authority, unexhausted. A parallel case might seem to be that of his great French contemporary Emile Durkheim, but in practice they are very different. I, to whom Durkheim is by far the greater sociologist, know perfectly well that Durkheim is dead and a part of the chronicles of my discipline, and this is true for the sociological profession as a whole. But Weber is only now settling into some sort of perspective and only now being sifted through so that we may take from him what is valuable and useful and discard what is disproved, what is a false lead, what is muddle, and what was always mistaken. The process is far from complete.

It is not as if Weber were a political prophet, the founder of a secular religion like Marx. I think, indeed, that he was more of an ideologist and is admired more for ideological reasons than is commonly supposed, but no one is or has been a Weberian in even the mildest of the senses in which one can say that someone is a Marxist. It is true that Weber is believed to be a great sociological diagnostician, a writer who can still tell us about the origins and essential essence of our industrial society and our dreadful, rewarding century. It is true that he is believed to reveal discomfiting and tragic tendencies in the movement of our society and our politics. It is true that he is in some ways typically and, both consciously and unawares, a revelatory German—

and Germany is a great and still enigmatic fact for Europe and the world. Because of his perplexities and his clarities Weber is both a guide and a clue to the enigmas of Germany in his own time, to the subsequent Nazi period, and to undecided issues of power and action in the present epoch. His fame, then, is bound up with his ambiguities, with the unadmitted or unexpressed belief that properly deciphered Weber would be found to conceal on his person the keys to both a specific society and to modern society at large.

If I may employ a metaphor and a phrase I have used before, sociology is a major form of human self-consciousness, a kind of imperfect looking glass in which we may see reflected back the visage of society as Perseus in the Greek tale saw the face of Medusa, that face which directly confronted turned men to stone. Sociology both makes society clear and present to us and makes society bearable and subject to analysis by endistancing us from the stark reality of immediate apprehension. It is this quality which gives sociology a public power far beyond anything one might expect from the very limited, though still valuable, nature of its actual achievement. The works of Weber, edited and put together in such large measure after his death, with their combination of learned gravity and romantic unction, and above all with their inconclusiveness and their suggestive contradictions, fulfill almost perfectly one public conception, secretly shared within the sociological profession, of the sociologist.

This would not be so true were he not mysterious. His great contemporaries in sociology were all gifted with clarity. I do not mean by this that they are easy writers. It is very difficult to provide easy reading about what is hard in content—and society is not simple—and it is probably impossible to deploy an elegant accessibility in one's prose on a difficult subject if one is also original. But Pareto, Durkheim, and Hobhouse are never mysterious. They may be wrong, they may be absurd, they may deceive themselves by bad argument, but they are not obscure. One knows what their problems are; one knows what they believe to be solutions. They may astonish us by insight and ingenuity and baffle us by naïveté, but they lead us through labyrinths. Weber leads us into labyrinths with no Ariadne's thread to aid our return. One can see this either as a merit, claiming that life and society really are like that, and that no one else has penetrated so far; or one can see it as a proof of failure, that failure which, as it is the defeat of great strength and great effort, is more honorable than success. I must admit a prejudice here which the reader should keep in mind in what follows: I prefer success to failure in science and scholarship, and while I admit that society is obscure and labyrinthine —what else?—that admission only strengthens my desire for clear charts, even if they honestly reveal areas still unexplored and the existence of precipices and rockfalls.

Finally, if we live in a thought-world which has been sociologized, we have to face another facet of Weber— that of the paradigmatic and exemplary sociologist. For a whole series of reasons, the reputation of Karl Marx has been reborn in a new form, the form of Marx as a sociologist. I believe that this is error: that Marx neither was—nor in a very important sense intended to be—a sociologist. But that is not an opinion which is widely shared. To those to whom Marxism is a sociology, Weber is the great antagonist. And since in all antagonism there is also complementarity, Marx and Weber as sociologists are seen as opposed twins, as archetypes. That error, at least, I hope these pages will correct.

The Life

● ●

ii

Max Weber was born in the town of Erfurt in Thuringia on April 21, 1864. Thuringia has now disappeared into the anonymity of the German Democratic Republic. But in 1864 it was a part of the Prussian dominion, of that power which perplexed and haunted Weber throughout his life. His family was defined by its Protestantism. His father's ancestors were Lutheran refugees from the Austrian empire who had gone to Bielefeld and become major cloth merchants. His mother's family traced itself back to Wilhelm von Wallenstein, a German who had served in the armies of the great Gustavus Adolphus, "Lion of the North and Bulwark of the Protestant Faith." The Wallensteins—spelled Fallenstein in Swedish—became intellectuals of a kind; schoolteachers or what in Scotland would be called dominies. One

of them—such was a common destiny for a dominie—
took to drink and deserted his Huguenot wife. His
son, G. F. Fallenstein, in turn underwent a period
of mental disorder, then became an apostle of German romantic nationalism and "folkishness" who, after
fighting Napoleon, joined the military police in the
occupied Paris of 1815 and, in the following year,
became a bureaucrat in Düsseldorf. In Paris this man
added to his romantic German nationalism and his
hatred for Napoleon an inconvenient attachment to
the libertarian ideas of the French Revolution. As a
result he did not advance in his profession in the suspi-
cious world of the restoration until 1832, when he
became state councilor (*Regierungsrat*) in Coblenz.
There in 1835 he married, for the second time, Emilia
Souchay, whose daughter Helene Fallenstein was to be
the mother of Max Weber.

The Souchays, too, had behind them a record as refugees of conscience, for they were by origin Calvinists
who had fled from Orléans after the revocation of religious tolerance to the Huguenots in 1685. In Frankfurt
they became successful merchants with branches of
their business in London and Manchester. Fallenstein
did well financially from the marriage and in 1842
moved to serve the Prussian government in Berlin. But
he did not succeed in his new job, and in 1847 he
retired to Heidelberg. There he occupied himself with
good works and in moving in learned circles dominated
by the historians Friedrich Schlosser and his pupil
Gervinus. This friendship was to be of importance to
the young Weber's destiny.

Schlosser was an opponent of the new "scientific"
history created by Ranke. No history, he held, could be

free from value-judgments and preconceptions arising out of nonhistorical considerations. The historian has the moral duty to judge men and events. History not only teaches itself but is also an ethical activity which forms the character of its students and of their public life. Gervinus, who was one of the seven Göttingen professors dismissed for constitutionalism by the Hanoverian monarchy, took part in the liberal Frankfurt Parliament of 1848, championed a federal Germany, and irreconcilably opposed Bismarck and the Hohenzollern imperium. Weber was to wrestle, inconclusively, with the problems set by these scholars all his life. But the influence of Gervinus was to be more than intellectual: it was to affect the familial, the sensual, and the psychological formation of Weber until the day of his death, for Gervinus lived on in the Fallenstein home after Fallenstein's death. He tried to seduce Helene, Weber's mother, and then tried to arrange a marriage for her with one of his students. She escaped to the home of her sister, wife of the historian Baumgarten, in Berlin, and there she met and married Max Weber *père*. She never overcame her dread of the sexual life, and the marriage was one of unhappiness, pietism, and complaint.

The man Helene married, born in 1836, was the youngest son of the Bielefeld Webers. His eldest brother transformed the cloth business by instituting a rationalized putting-out[1] system and flourished mightily as entrepreneur. The youngest brother, by training a

---

[1] "Putting-out system": in the English and European cloth industries factory production was preceded by domestic production, centrally organized (and marketed) by local businessmen.

lawyer, became after taking his doctorate both a civic employee and a journalist in Berlin. He was an ardent monarchist and Bismarckian. He went to Erfurt as a magistrate and then, after the birth of his son, came back to Berlin to pursue a minor but successful career in Prussian politics. Commentators have described his opinions as liberal: in no country but Hohenzollern Prussia could agreement with Heinrich von Treitschke or men like him be taken as a proof of liberalism. Yet the error about the politics of Max Weber *père* is in one way comprehensible. Imperial Germany developed no genuinely conservative party. The new Empire was always in some ways a power wherein legitimacy could not flow from the wisdom of the past, be a continuation of the *mos maiorum*. The Bismarckian "National Liberals" to whom the elder Weber attached himself defined politics by the state, not society, and its state was the established order of Prussia. This was, as we shall see, by no means the same thing as the established order of the new, unified Germany.

Nor was Weber's father merely *l'homme moyen sensuel*, even if that is how his wife saw him. He was a part of that new nineteenth-century world of newspapers and journals, of the politics of large franchises and narrow powers, of gossip, news, and knowledge of what went on in the corridors of power—of parliaments, of government offices, of party headquarters, of newspaper administrations, and of a court. His moral principles were those of an "ethic of success," not of intrinsic merit. The dichotomy was to haunt the son, but as a young man he followed his father's judgment. The father's circle was intellectual in a narrow sense: professors of history counted for much in it, but a concern with creativity, with beauty, with criticism as a torturing passion, with novelty, were not part of it. This world of Rickert, Sybel, and Treitschke was intellectual, but also Philistine. In it Weber's father would bear nothing pushed to extremes, no public reasoning, no course of action followed to the end: he was a man much at ease in Zion; publicly complaisant and privately demanding, expecting much of others. In this expectation neither father nor son, each in his own way, was greatly to be disappointed.

To all this Helene Fallenstein-Weber was opposed. Sex, we may feel, was, as it is so often, her weapon in the war of the sexes. If Marianne Weber, Max's wife, is to be believed, her mother-in-law Helene hated sexuality: the marriage-bed was a place of sorrow and of sin; only procreation could justify that union of bodies from which age would bring a merciful release. What this meant to the elder Weber one can, with sympathy, imagine. From 1876 on, the relations of Weber's parents were those of an institutionalized estrangement. The picture is a familiar one to any student of the nineteenth century. As is usual in this picture, the Webers had numerous children; and as is also usual in that age, they were familiar with the deaths of children. Helene Weber used the frail health and the danger of death of her eldest son as a criticism and a weapon against a father who was also not to be forgiven for the death of an infant daughter.

Helene was devout in her own way. In the issues of religion her mind was decided. She sought God personally, not through rites or theology. She did not seek Him emotionally, but in a conduct of quiet, decisive religiosity. She was much moved by that New England preaching of the nineteenth century which, etiolating Christianity and Calvinism, refusing the drama, the terror, the splendor, and the order, advocated a resolved repudiation of emotion and desire combined with a narrow individualism and the finding of uncomfortable duty in the daily round. In a way this goes back to an old theme, influential in Britain and America, developed by Calvinists in the seventeenth century and to be found at work in the shorter catechism of the Church of Scotland but not, I think, in either Calvin or Knox. It is the idea that the sanctification of the individual is a process exemplified in the dutiful collaboration in God's work practiced by the unfallen Adam in Eden and, after the Fall, offered to those who work in their calling by the Covenant of Grace. But to Helene Weber, reading the divines of nineteenth-century America, this teaching was cut from its roots, humanized, quietized, and rationalized by two hundred years of history. It was powerfully to affect the thinking of her son.

When Helene had run off from Heidelberg to Berlin she took refuge as a seventeen-year-old girl with her elder sister Ida, whose husband, Hermann Baumgarten, was later to be yet another influence on the young Max. Baumgarten was an enemy of exactly those things and men to which Max Weber senior was much attached. He thought nothing of the eloquent, vulgar, and moving Treitschke, and, in criticizing Treitschke, he criticized by implication Prussia and the Hohenzollern dynasty. He had believed, like all his generation, in a unification of the German states, but not in the unification that he found. His attitudes, carried into the period after 1871, were largely those of Gervinus. Baumgarten therefore withdrew from the political order to preach a history conducted without party zeal and to condemn the Bismarckian empire as both unstable and unwise in its cults of war and power and its rejection of any true parliamentarianism. A nonpolitical attitude of this kind, publicly expressed, is of course itself a kind of politics.

Weber's aunt, Ida Baumgarten, took a religious position close to that of Helene Weber, but unlike Helene she was an overtly dominant person in her home. She exercised an obtrusive charity, proclaiming the primacy of Christian duty. Weber was to find in her home both a puzzle and a challenge at a crucial period of his career when, as a conscript, he was stationed in Strasbourg, the capital of German-occupied Alsace. The politics and the religion of the Baumgartens were incorporated in the antinomies of his thought as a young man. Yet in a sense they had been present throughout his childhood. Not all the currents of Germany flowed into his early life—the workers and the nobles were not there—but there was enough in this materially comfortable, intense, yet Philistine milieu to catch him forever in a net of inherited and contemporary contradiction. His sociology is, among other things, the record of his attempt to escape that net.

Let us now look at the formal facts of his career. They appear simple enough. At the age of two he was ill—undoubtedly very ill, though one may doubt the diagnosis of meningitis—and became the particular object of his mother's brooding concern. In 1869 the family resettled in Berlin in the Charlottenburg district and Weber went to school there, receiving an orthodox, mainly classical education. In 1882 he went to Heidel-

berg and entered the law faculty. In 1884 he was at
Strasbourg as a (conscript) junior officer. In 1884–1885
he was at Berlin as a student, and 1885–1886 at Göttingen. (In the German university system, there was
nothing unusual in this story of movement from place
to place.) After leaving Göttingen he spent over three
years holding a minor legal position in Berlin, preparing
his doctoral thesis, and returning briefly as a reserve
officer to Strasbourg (he also served in the same capacity
in Posen). He took his doctorate with a thesis *On the
History of Medieval Trading Companies* in 1889. He
was now an "assessor" in the lower courts of Berlin. In
1891 he qualified as a university teacher with a thesis
on *The Agricultural History of Rome in Its Relation to
Public and Private Law.* (It was at the examination of
this thesis that the great historian Theodor Mommsen
said, "When I must descend to the grave I would hap-
pily say to no one but the highly-to-be-esteemed Max
Weber, 'My son, here is my lance which is become too
heavy for my arm.'") In 1892 Weber got a minor position teaching law in Berlin and, in the same year, married his second cousin on his father's side. In 1894 the
University of Freiburg im Breisgau gave him a chair in
political economy. In 1897 he succeeded the economist
Karl Knies at Heidelberg. A "nervous breakdown" followed, and in 1899 he was given leave to recover himself. He traveled in Europe—England, Scotland,
Belgium, Italy—and the United States. In 1903 Weber,
along with Werner Sombart and Philipp Jaffé, founded
the journal *Archiv für Sozialwissenschaft und Sozialpolitik.* During the 1914–1918 war he worked in hospital administration. 1918 saw him return to teaching in a
specially created chair of sociology in Vienna. In 1919

he took over the chair previously held by another famous economist, Lujo Brentano, in Munich. As described earlier, he died the following year. Except for the prolonged "breakdown" it is a typical enough story of academic life, but that exception is a large one. One can only admire and perhaps approve that element in the German university system which allowed a man, however distinguished and intellectually productive, to abjure teaching for twenty years.

Before we look more closely at the personal life, three attachments should be mentioned, attachments at once academic and political. One of these was to the Evangelical Social Union (Evangelisch-Soziale Verein), a Protestant body which represented something of the same reaction to industrial and urban society in its birth pangs as Christian Socialism and its successors in England and the Social Gospel movement in the United States. The Union was concordant in its views with the attitudes of his mother and of the Baumgartens. It was an attempt to make faith and charity relevant by social welfare and social administration to a transformed society. Weber was a founding member from 1890 onward and through his membership became associated with the politician and publicist Friedrich Naumann.

Older and more distinguished (it dated from 1872) was the Social Political Union (Verein für Sozialpolitik), one of the most important of all the learned societies in the history of the social sciences. In its early days the Social Political Union advanced views on social policy, but after 1881 and the Bismarckian provisions in the field of social assurance it concerned itself not with propaganda but with research and discussion among academics. For nearly all of Weber's period of membership (1888–1920), the dominant figure in the Union was Gustav Schmoller, who, on the whole, steered its concerns away from technical and theoretical economics and kept its sights on an approach, by way of social and economic history, to questions of society. The Union was a spur to the early researches of Weber and a platform for his opinions and polemics. It would be absurd to regard the Union as nonpolitical after its change of policy in 1881, for its researches were guided not by disinterested science, by problems arising from the inner development of the social sciences, but always by issues of public choice, alarm, or decision. I do not mean that this was somehow through unconscious choice and interest: it was direct and deliberate.

Thirdly, there was the National Liberal Party. Though certainly national, the liberalism of this body might not have been recognized elsewhere in Europe. It was the party of the elder Max Weber, who was a member of both the Prussian Diet and the imperial parliament, or Reichstag. In religion as in politics, Weber was always ambiguous. For all his concern with questions of faith and Christian charity he was, as he put it, "religiously unmusical." About political parties he was positively slippery and not, one feels, merely from a desire to maintain an academic and poised objectivity. His doubts about the National Liberals are evident even when he was only twenty-three. Yet to the problems of German politics he constantly brought National Liberal attitudes so that, for example, he could support—yet ambiguously criticize—the National Liberals' acceptance of Bismarck's antisocialist laws. Even in the sudden liberation of defeat from 1918–1920 the ambiguities and the attitudes remain, even though Weber appears to be, at the last, politically committed as man and citizen. One can ascribe, if one wishes, a great deal of Weber's political flirtations—not so much adultery as adulteration—both to the real difficulties of his time and place, and, secondly, to the scruples of a mind delicately aware of all the threads and knots of consideration that are the web of politics. It seems to me, given those matters on which he was clear and unambiguous, that this is to do him altogether too much justice. And of course we should remember that some of such blame as there is does not really belong to Weber but to those writers who since his death have worked to make him a modern master not only of thought and learning but of political attitude and action.

The Man

iii

The man who lived out his life in the tangle of family influence, public affairs, and academic work is curiously elusive. Even about his mature physical appearance there are puzzles. Weber was tall, burly, heavily bearded, and appeared stern. His speech, we are told, was simple and direct, yet also flexibly geared to the personality he was addressing. He is always pictured full-face, and I have been told—truly or not I cannot tell—that he objected to any representation in profile which might reveal the conformation of his nose. For his face was scarred from dueling accidents, and his features made heavy by much beer-drinking in his student days—his mother slapped his face on first seeing her coarsened son on his return from the university. Weber gave an impression of poise, confidence, and earnestness but also, to a sensitive observer like the psychiatrist and philosopher Karl Jaspers, of contained tension, embodied schism.

There is, I have long felt, some justice in Wilhelm Reich's idea that character is a coat of mail donned by men in our civilization as a defense against the impulses of desire, of attraction and repulsion. This armor is itself a kind of social and historical product, and is not only a protection but also a prerequisite for some kinds of aggression. If we take this metaphor seriously, then Weber wore an armor of character which was both unusually heavy and restricting and unusually irksome to the tender flesh within. Weber's carapace was certainly so chafing, so ponderous that at times he found it unbearable.

His sensual and aesthetic life was restricted. He drank and dueled as a student in the Corps of the Alemanni. At the same time, his wife tells us, he remained chaste. His first love affair with one of the Baumgartens seems sad, tepid, and pure. His marriage with his relative Marianne Schnitzer was perhaps never consummated, and he wrote to her both of his constant struggle to endure and to domesticate his "elemental passions" and also of his "natural sobriety" as something which unfitted him for love. Not surprisingly, he had a number of sentimental friendships with women throughout his life. But in his later years when he moved in more bohemian circles, intellectual rather than academic, he appears to have enjoyed a releasing and happy affair. (Again I have been told, but do not know how accurately, that he went to Vienna toward the end of the war not for the intellectual reasons which are suggested by most writers but to be near a new love.) Weber was deeply involved with his brothers and perhaps in some of his concerns we can find a certain substitute for paternity. There is to me something odd in the intermarriage and interbreeding of the academic and bourgeois clan to which he belonged—a pattern to which he contributed by his own marriage.[1]

The aesthetic world was one to which his relation remains puzzling. As a boy he is said to have steeped himself in the Greek and Roman classics; but their influence, save as source materials for economic, legal, and (rarely) political study, is not apparent. Like all good Germans he knew his Goethe—and disliked his aesthetic hedonism—and he praised Schiller. But German literature seems hardly to have touched his young mind as an active influence. Of his great near contemporaries we can find him, unsurprisingly, casting dilemmas into forms and situations derived from Ibsen, the greatest of all dramatists of the Protestant ethic. And we know that Nietzsche powerfully influenced him, particularly in the last fifteen years or so of his life, but I can see no sign that this influence had any aesthetic resonance, which it undoubtedly had on Weber's brilliant contemporary in German sociology, Georg Simmel. In the great age of the arts which was to flower most fully in the German-speaking lands after 1918 but which begins in the 1890s, Weber moves blindly even when he is associated with the circle around the symbolist poet Stefan George—about whom Simmel wrote and who was admired by Weber even before they had met. It is indeed

[1] Such clans are to be found in most countries. They form distinct subcultures and do much to further their members' careers in the higher education apparatus. Their dynamics deserve study.

understandable that Weber was not at home in this antiacademic hothouse of sometimes perverse emotion and individual adulation, yet the release of spirit so evident in his later years clearly owed much to these stumbling contacts. His aesthetic incapacity seems to me both willed and inherited: willed as inappropriate to the seriousness and depth of the scholar, inherited as a consequence of the pietism and philistinism of his family background.

I do not know how far Weber was a man for whom the visual world existed. His travel letters from Scotland, for example, are full of conventional appreciations of landscape, but it is a mistake to think that conventional responses are necessarily either false or mistaken. His writings on music are learned and suggestive, but unusually obscure and related to what is perhaps the central theme of all his thought, the rationalization, secularization, and demythologizing of the human world. One would not need to care for music to write thus, but to *choose* to do so is surely significant.

These matters may seem remote from a concern with Weber's central interests. Yet if I am right about him, they are in fact very relevant. Durkheim in France so defined his sociological concerns that the emotive, sensual, and aesthetic spheres are not central to his effort at an understanding of how society is possible. Weber's strategy, however, should permit no such exclusion, and as a result his defects and rejections in these sectors of existence flaw his total achievement and put much of it in question. Yet, as so often, one feels exactly here a contained tension, an unstated polarity in all he does. We are close to his essential enigma.

No one has written of Weber without talking of

tension, of unresolved, perhaps agonizing contradictions. Could he have found relief in action rather than
in study and in thought? Throughout his life he recurs
to his capacity for a *vita activa*, the merits of and the
need for such a life. Yet he always draws back from it
until his fiftieth year. He dramatizes this need throughout his life, but it seems mere dramatization until 1914.
Many dons go on like this; discontented with the *vita
contempliva* they express themselves violently and curse
the acedia which is the occupational disease of their
trade. Certainly Weber enjoyed himself hugely in his
work as an administrator of nine major and forty minor
hospital units during World War I. He drove his car—
known as the "yellow peril"—furiously from place to
place, and his duties delighted him and were well performed. He conventionally regretted not being a fighter
—he seems quite to have enjoyed and to have valued his
military service and his role as reserve officer—and expressed the extraordinary wish that the war should have
come twenty-five years earlier, which, he contended,
would have been the right time for it. (One can only
ask, why?) His fascination with power and force, common enough in the Europe of his day, still seems excessive and sickly. Action may well discharge tension: but
is tension always something that is best discharged?

All of which takes us to the nature of the prolonged
"breakdown." The young Weber worked prodigiously
hard. His academic output down to 1893 is enormous in
learning, range, and volume. True, he was financially
secure, but he resented his financial dependence on his
family and was extremely ambitious for academic and
public advancement. His early work is therefore both
scholarly and directed to issues of public policy, above

all to the agrarian problems of Prussia's eastern marches, the world of the Junkers and the subordinate Slavs. And in these years he was changing his domestic allegiances. To put it crudely, he was changing from being his father's to being his mother's son. The worldly, compliant, and relaxed father who appeared in public was something of a domestic tyrant who suffered from the fact—not in itself surely without reward—that his earnings did not equal his wife's inherited income. I have mentioned their sexual incompatibility, but there was beyond that a disdain for his wife's pieties and charity. It is difficult not to believe that the father represented not just a domestic despotism but also the imperial state, Philistine and bullying, of which he was a pillar. The attitudes of Max Weber, at once admiring, obedient, and dissident, to the German state surely reflect and continue his attitudes to his father. At the same time he longed for the reform or ending of that state yet found in it an admirable strength.

The elder Max Weber died in 1897 and the period of the son's breakdown followed. One is inclined to use an old piece of jargon and say that it is no accident that Weber's sociology and political thinking recur again and again to the themes of patriarchalism, patrimonialism, and authority. To use a necessary argot, he attempted to internalize in his own personality those strong qualities of the German state which he both admired and dreaded, and those moral commitments, severed from the tree of religious life, which were the core of his mother's being. For perhaps seven weeks before the father's death, he and his son had been locked in dispute. The quarrel was a family one: should the father live in Heidelberg with his wife and son? The

desire does not seem surprising and the quarrel dispro-
portionate. Anyhow, shortly after his father's funeral
Weber became ill, apparently recovered, and did some
lecturing for the Evangelical Social Union, but by May
1898 he had become insomniac, walked weeping in the
spring woods, and was hospitalized. From then on brief
recoveries, with the torture—as he found it—of teaching, followed in a deepening succession. His mother, in
the Calvinist tradition, was unimpressed: her son
should "pull himself together." In 1900 he began a leave
without terminal date from the university.

For three years he traveled in Europe. In 1902, however, Weber felt able once again to read and to work,
even if lightly, and in 1903 he undertook along with
Werner Sombart the editorship of a learned journal, the
*Archiv für Sozialwissenschaft und Sozialpolitik (Social
Science and Social Political Archives)*. In 1904 he
visited America, on an invitation to the Louisiana Purchase Exposition at Saint Louis, traveling as far as
Oklahoma and New Orleans, impressed everywhere by
the force and the brutality of American capitalism and
a political order in which the concomitant of democracy was machine politics, city bossism, and efficient,
bureaucratic party organization. In these years of
"breakdown" he wrote furiously out of an extended
knowledge and concern for the world. He was becoming truly a sociologist, not a jurist or an economist, and
by 1909 he was publicly committed to sociology as a
discipline and to membership in the new German Sociological Society (Deutsche Gesellschaft für Soziologie),
a body of active and committed scholarship under the
presidency of the venerable Ferdinand Tönnies. Yet
officially he was still an invalid, and, though his world

and health expanded in the immediate prewar years to include new friends and new concerns, his liberation from the burdens of a wounded mind really began only with the war of 1914 and became complete with the fall of the Empire in 1918 and with Weber's final desertion of his monarchist principles. The death of the state may be said to have completed the cure of a malaise precipitated by the death of his father.

One should not view the years from 1904 onward as a time of mere hypochondria. In the few letters in Weber's own tiny, crabbed hand which I have personally examined from this period one finds his difficult script becoming more obscure and irregular just as he himself and those who wrote about him report fresh attacks and recurrences of ill-health. Yet there is a sense in which the illnesses and hypochondrias, the mysterious ailments and nervous crises that an earlier stage of medical science so freely permitted its more prosperous patients, were protective. Today we might well set about curing a Thomas Carlyle, a Herbert Spencer, a Charles Darwin, a Max Weber: as a result we might also make their mature work impossible. Illness is no longer a licit defense against the importunities of the world knocking at the door of the artist or scholar. We have become puritanical about health: to be ill, which was then an alternative vocation for the comfortably off, is now a source of guilt and even of condemnation. One cannot go back and diagnose Weber, though certain hypotheses seem inescapable, but it does appear likely that without his breakdown we would not have or know, even in its fragmentary form, the work to which he owes his present fame and influence. The strength of the German academic system that could allow Weber his prolonged leave, his "titular" chair, his ambiguity of field—he can be thought of as lawyer, historian, economist, philosopher, political scientist as well as sociologist—is today nowhere to be found. In it Weber could take advantage of his real sufferings and turn them to the advancement of learning.

He had one other advantage in his relative financial security. The dynamics of his clan, with its intermarriages, consolidated rather than dispersed family capital in a world of stable currencies and low taxation. The private scholar—and that is what Weber in part was—could flourish modestly in the Europe of the nineteenth and early twentieth century. The institutionalized and bureaucratic research of our age would have almost no place for him. The economies of our time, so much richer in so many ways, hardly permit such existence. To ask, as I have heard it put, for a new Max Weber to redeem modern sociology is to ask what is institutionally, economically, and culturally impossible in the Europe of the late twentieth century. Weber was, as is true of us all, but was particularly true of him, a man of his time and society; not merely because he unavoidably embodied and expressed something of the spirit of his age, but because he lived in a Europe that specifically permitted his individual style of life and work.

The Country

●

IV

The most remarkable thing about Weber's Europe is that it was at peace and remained so for forty-three years after the signing (in the Swan Hotel in Frankfurt) of the treaty which brought to an end the Franco-Prussian War. Of course, the powers of Europe waged wars in other continents; of course and in particular in southeastern Europe there were wars and revolts in which the greater powers intervened. But there was no war which engaged the major powers against one another. If much of the responsibility for the outbreak of war in 1914 must lie with the German Empire, it is equally true that it was that Empire which had by diplomacy, threat, and ingenuity done much to maintain the longest peace Europe has known in the history of its state system. German arms had created a new

Europe; the fear of these arms helped to maintain it.

The German state was very odd, and there has been nothing quite like it before or since. It is this oddity that makes Weber in my judgment less significant as a political thinker than is usually believed or than he might have been. The other new polities of his age, the Third French Republic and the Kingdom of Italy, are full of political instruction for any student of modern representative government, and if that instruction is not always edifying it is very human, and thus valuable. But the German state was a mishmash; it was at once a dynasty, a federation, a representative system, a despotism, an army, a bureaucracy, and a colonial regime. The dynasty of the Hohenzollerns did not possess a separate historical dignity like the Habsburg *domus Austriae*, but it was nonetheless of great weight, for the dynasty had powers and loyalties which were large if ill-defined. It was possible, it was even usual, for men like Weber to approve the monarchist principle and condemn the monarch who was at once Emperor, Commander-in-Chief, and King of Prussia and open to criticism in all three roles as well as personally. The federation too was a reality, not a façade, but the will of Prussia was its core and Prussia could outvote all the rest of the federation's members. In it the three free northern ports, the seventeen dukedoms, and the other three kingdoms possessed real but subordinate wills. Weber's mind moved always in the orbit of the dominant, Prussian will.

The representative system is too complex for its exploration to be worth space in an account of Weber, even though Weber loved to play at constitution-making. The German Empire's constituent states typically were bicameral, with an aristocratic upper house and a lower chamber elected by universal manhood suffrage. In Prussia the three-tier electoral regime kept power in the hands of the landowners and men of the Right. The imperial parliament (*Reichstag*) stood ambiguously to the Chancellor of the Empire, who could claim to be responsible not to it but to the Kaiser. The Army estimates were indeed renewed by the Reichstag but only every seventh year, so that the Chancellor had a motive for alarm and bellicosity at regular intervals. Yet all in all Kaiser and Chancellor were despotically situated in relation to the legislative and executive powers of the state. To the Army, the most powerful force in all that world, their will was central. Every man was a soldier and thus a subordinate in the one formative role which attached him to the one certainly national and glorious institution of the society. How far was he also a citizen? Weber hardly examined this situation. One must assume that he accepted it and its consequences.

The German state was, of course, a bureaucracy. The fame of that civil service, orderly and efficient, is very great. Yet it was not unique, and Austria-Hungary, with less fuss, had a very loyal and efficient bureaucracy. Similarly, it is a commonplace that the continuity in the history of the French state is the continuity of its administrators. And the imperial Indian Civil Service probably did more, better, with smaller resources than any other bureaucracy in history. Yet somehow it is assumed that the civil services of the German Empire were peculiarly exemplary. Certainly these services regulated more things in more detail than in other lands; and Weber never questioned the paradigmatic character of the system, while his fellow countrymen accorded it a respect and an obedience to be found nowhere else in Europe. What is more, it was only in imperial Russia that so wide a range of professions and vocations were included within the categories of public service. Elsewhere, societies were more diverse and centers of countervailing power were to be found in a complex of associations and free professions. Through the Army and the bureaucracy, the state in Germany extended uniquely far into the fabric of ordinary life. Weber's reputation rightly depends in large measure on his work as diagnostician of the bureaucratic order; his opportunities, where the state through its administrative apparatus claimed such omnicompetence, for undertaking a clinical study of bureaucracy were uniquely great.

In its eastern and western marches Germany was a colonial power. Alsace-Lorraine was a *Reichsland*, an area of imperial administration (a destiny which Weber thought during much of the war perfectly suitable for a good deal of conquered western Europe). In the east the Prussian heritage to Germany of largely Slav territories ruled by landed aristocracy, depending too on immigrant non-German labor, represented an older kind of colonialism. How could the Empire do with or do without these non-German peasants and coal miners? Could Prussia exist without its eastern lords, those Junkers who in large measure *were* Prussia but who ruled and exploited the non-Germans? Here was a contradiction in the heart of the ideology of the Empire: its claims to legitimacy were largely those of common speech and blood, of national self-determination, of "folkishness," but Prussia, the major constituent of the Empire, was a regime of caste and of rule over aliens. Weber's career as sociologist emerged directly out of his engagement with these problems.

Weber was strictly and in both the Marxist and non-Marxist senses a bourgeois, a man of the upper, trading orders of urban life. The world of the soil and the world of the aristocracy were alien to him. The world of the latter was the dream of the bourgeoisie: Germans had made no Declaration of the Rights of Man and the Citizen, they had indulged in no Putney Debates, far less executed anointed kings. Walther Rathenau, Jewish industrialist, patriot, and statesman, once told the German upper middle classes that they would never dàre to push their principles or their politics *à outrance*, for they loved and feared a system in which one might oneself receive a patent of nobility, enter an upper chamber, or see one's son officially advanced. The aristocratic fact was a central source of the unpolitical politics of Weber's class. Rathenau was right.

In such a regime the daily business of politics was inevitably stultifying, arbitrary, likely to run into the sands or be swept by whirlwinds. The political structure was too irrational, complex, and arbitrary for either a healthy practice or a profound political science. Fears were magnified, hopes turned on individuals and hypotheses about individuals and situations, so that Germany was not a political laboratory such as Tocqueville had found in America, but a witches' cauldron from which even a Weber could derive only ambiguous prophecy, alarm, and a faltering, irresolute will.

But in no polity, however authoritarian—and imperial Germany is not to be confused with the authoritarian states of modern times—is the state coterminous with the society. Weber's society, regarded as a nation, may have lacked a civic culture, but it contained in its constituent parts local traditions in which both civic culture and civic courage could be found. This localism was not favored in the Empire, and it concerned Weber, a mobile member of the academic profession, very little. As a result his diagnoses of actual situations tended to extremes and to polarizations. What is more, Weber as a Protestant failed to appreciate properly that nearly 40 per cent of the population were Catholics. Weber's extensive writings on religion in Europe and Asia start from a Protestant point of judgment and tacitly accept the proposition that the Protestant and the German spirits are one.

This belief was a commonplace of the age, but one we must remember when we look at what Weber had to say about Protestantism and capitalism. Not merely was the official ideology of the dynasty Protestant, but throughout America, England, and Germany wealth, power, and valor were supposed to be correlated with reformed Christianity. Sometimes this correlation was referred for explanation to some independent biological merit of the Teutonic peoples, and sometimes Protestantism was itself regarded as the cause of wealth and power as well as being also their reward. Bismarck's struggle with the Catholic Church in Germany, from 1871 to 1887, could be understood—and was understood—to be at once national and economically progressive. So Protestantism was at once sacred history and the wave of the future.

Progress was above all conceived to be economic. Although certain parts of the *Reich* had industrialized early in the nineteenth century, the Empire as a whole was in the late nineteenth century a state moving into advanced industrial capitalism at breakneck speed. Only in the post-bellum United States could anything similar be found. The railway network was completed. The iron of Lorraine fed the new mills and factories. The French war indemnity provided a new source for investment. German industry was from its foundations large-scale and technologically advanced, and in fields like heavy chemicals it led the world. The great banks flourished in this situation of new demands and opportunities. Rationalization was the order of the day; a single capital market—Weber was much interested in stock exchanges, making a special study of that in Glasgow—a single currency, a single system of weights and measures, and a single code of industrial and commercial law served and were served by the new order of rational gain. Corporations multiplied. Weber witnessed the creation of an industrial society.

And he saw also the creation of a new scale and style of urban life. The old, traditional Germany of petty towns and petty dignitaries, all linked to small trade and closely bound to rural markets and supplies, was becoming a country of great cities—the very word *Großstadt* was invented to describe them—of which Berlin with its 4 million inhabitants was the chief. By 1900 only about 20 per cent of the Germans lived in country areas. These great cities were places of bankers, bureaucrats, and traders, of skilled professions and clerks, but most of all they were the homes of a new working class. As the total population grew, surpassing that of England or France in numbers, although also significantly younger, this working class increased disproportionately. It seemed as though the new cities were fulfilling the implied predictions of Marx not merely in moving into industrial capitalism but in polarizing Germany into two antagonistic sectors of which the workers formed the larger group. In thirty years the trade unions multiplied their numbers nearly ten times, so that in 1914 they had over 3 million members. The socialists, persecuted by Bismarck, still grew in strength and represented, it appeared, radically new principles of party organization, so that radical hopes were carried forward by bureaucratic mass politics based on the towns. To come to grips with the city and its politics was therefore a central challenge to Weber's understanding of society. It is probably fair to say—and a judgment on the progress of the social sciences over the fifty years since Weber's death—that no one has better grasped the social nature of modern urbanism since his time.

Save in the military sphere, where union was imposed and gladly accepted, German society in Weber's period presents a picture of incoherence and competing force matched in no other European country. Nor were the jarring forces so locked that any kind of stability resulted; rather, all was uncertain and shifting in the dynamism of enormous energy and ceaseless change which characterized Germany. That at the cultural level there were profound continuities was something that a century of often terrible history has taught us, but the importance and inertia of these cultural factors were things inevitably invisible to Weber's generation. Indeed, it seemed possible that men were being atomized, separated from their fellows, their society, and their past, and that only a fragmented mass would remain. In all this turmoil of growth there was a sense of an ending, a twilight beyond which lay what night, what dawn?

Bismarck himself wrote that in "our parliamentary parties the real point of crystallization is not a program but a man, a parliamentary *condottiere*." As early as the 1890s Weber saw in the rootless middle classes and the fragmented masses a "longing for a new Caesar." The peace lasted forty-three years, but these years were felt to be precarious, and it is surely not too fanciful to find in Weber's nervous questing, his raids, often in depth, into so many territories of the mind, a reflection not of his character alone but of the perplexities of his age and country. War or a new Caesar—or some union of the two—might at least give some ease to these frets in the resolution of obedience and sacrifice. But these possibilities in their turn raised new questions and new fears. Only the pace of change continued unabated, and the fragmented world stayed for no answer.

The World of Learning

V

It was in the nineteenth century that knowledge became an industry. It was in the German universities that this industry was perfected. Knowledge is, of course, a social and public enterprise. It depends not only on study and discovery but also on criticism. For a subject to exist in the world of knowledge there has to be a community of scholars of that subject, communicating with each other, judging by common standards each other's work. Knowledge is then, and on the whole, cumulative—though the power of institutionalized forgetfulness in the world of learning should never be underestimated. To be engaged in the knowledge industry is thus to be involved in a kind of progress. By way of learned societies, books and journals, laboratories and libraries, teaching positions allowing time for discovery and expecting publication by their holders, learning becomes an institution of society. Learning in a particular subject (and even the advancement of knowledge), once that subject is institutionalized does not demand talent, far less genius, so much as orthodox labor. The laborers undergo a kind of apprenticeship and, increasingly following the German pattern, are expected to produce a masterpiece in its original sense —that is, a sample of decent academic work as an entitlement, usually marked by the conferring of the doctorate, to engage in advanced teaching and research. The process is very similar to that of the craft-apprentice earning the right to full membership in a master's guild.

Now sociology in the late nineteenth century was not —as it is now—institutionalized in this way. There was not, except in the United States, and even there only in a rather thin form, a community of sociologists in university positions and proudly legitimated by an appropriate training. The subject had, indeed, a long and ragged history. Retrospectively but accurately the activities of Montesquieu in France and of Ferguson in Scotland could be called sociological. The word itself had been invented by Comte in France and he had worked out a program for it and awarded the study of society a unique and privileged position as the crown of all the previously developed sciences. Few people had agreed. Neither the contents nor the methods of the enterprise were unambiguously defined. The activity of sociology was taken to be subversive in that it inevitably, by the mere fact of enquiry, questioned the existing state of social affairs. In the hands of Comte subversion went deeper, for to him sociology was not merely a study but a program of reform—and as an ideology Comtean sociology had little popular or official appeal for Europe, though it was in fact to be politically influential in South America and elsewhere. What was more, the word sociology was connected by many with socialism and the subject consequently condemned on the principle of guilt by association. The greatest nineteenth-century sociologist, Herbert Spencer, was neither educated in a university nor employed by one for all his ingenious and powerful defense of free market capitalism.

The first major work of German sociology appeared in 1887. Its author, Ferdinand Tönnies, lived most of his life without attaining to a university chair, yet *Community and Association (Gemeinschaft und Gesellschaft)* is still, rightly, read, and Tönnies is still a living influence on social thought. His younger contemporary, Weber, therefore was fortunate in that he gained academic advancement in other fields before becoming unequivocally committed to sociology, just as sociology as an institutionalized discipline has been fortunate in being able to claim for itself the legitimacy given by Weber's work and name.

History and the historical approach were the great German specialisms. German historians had established new canons of rigor in the use of sources, new standards of accuracy in exposition, and new modes of barbarity in academic prose. Everything was viewed from the standpoint of history, and it was believed that the central meaning of understanding was historical and developmental. To know the origins of a thing was to possess that thing. Thus law was to be grasped by the twin historical studies: first, of Roman law and its European reception in the sixteenth century; and second, by the yet more important study of the historical evolution of the legal customs and codes of the Teutonic barbarians and their medieval transformation. Again philology vindicated the historical method by researches that were comparative and inductive as well as historical. Even economics in Germany was more and more made subject to history, at the cost of lagging far behind what was achieved in pure analysis in Britain, France, and Austria, but with the gain of the construction of a viable discipline of economic history. The intellectual atmosphere breathed by the young Weber was saturated with history.

The achievement was genuine and great, and we are all in its debt. Weber belonged to what was probably the first European generation that could command with confidence a vast range of reliable secondary sources. True, these sources were mainly historical, but their accuracy, even as the mechanical products of the knowledge industry, was exemplary and their range enormous. Weber had good secondary sources not merely for the classical (primarily Roman) world and Europe but also for his studies of China, India, and ancient Palestine. Nothing is more stupid or vulgar than to blame either Weber or subsequent sociologists for often relying on and making use of the projects and results of the industry of historical knowledge. After all, what else is that industry for?

I think, in fact, that there is more than one good answer to that question, but surely such a utilization of these secondary sources is as good and legitimate as any other. No one expects a physicist or chemist to do each and every piece of research over again before using the results reported in the learned journals. Surely the human studies can proceed similarly, and Weber is to be envied rather than condemned for belonging to an age when such a utilization of the work of others was possible. Two matters, however, are worrying. Weber was blind to an alternative approach to data which was developed by Spencer in England and advanced by Durkheim in France. Secondly, he was intoxicated by the detail of his sources and frequently bemused by a historical attitude of mind into a forgetfulness of his original purposes in embarking on a particular study. He was also unfortunate, in my judgment—which on this matter is not widely shared—in getting involved in the German intellectual crisis about the nature and validity of historical knowledge itself.

The trouble here was a consequence of his sense that rigor in method was not enough, and that unless history could be shown to have foundations in accord with the criteria set by philosophy and logic, its claim to be even a valid form of knowledge—far less the most valid form —could not be sustained. If that claim fell, then German historiography was devalued, and the position of the other human sciences, all of which were supposed to be essentially historical, was put in the gravest doubt. These worries were compounded by a set of interlinked problems about values. Could a historian (or sociologist, etc.) avoid the intrusion of his own values into his work? Should he do so? Even if he should and could do so in his own specific work, must the very choice of an area or problem for study not inevitably involve him in a decision that demanded a valuation of problems one against another? Even at the conscious level these could seem grave issues, but there was worse.

The late nineteenth century has been called the age

of the discovery of the irrational and the unconscious. This is not quite true: irrationality is an old issue for thinkers and an older realization of poets and story-tellers. The unconscious has a long history, too; before Freud, in the German-speaking countries, there had been the philosophies of the unconscious of Schopen-hauer and Hartmann. If, however, it was now recog-nized with a special poignancy that all men, even scholars, were frequently irrational in their behavior and were moved by unconscious forces—implanted how in their being?—then did it not follow that all science, but most particularly perhaps the social sciences, were called in question? And sociology itself also raised very sharply the possibility that all scholarship was tainted, penetrated by values, distorted by the very constraints and interests of social life itself. Weber demanded of himself, in a time when these things were widely felt but not yet always precisely formulated, rigorous answers to these issues, a hard and unambiguous solu-tion to these uncertainties. How could a social science be established that was strong enough to accept that a presuppositionless history was impossible, and to deal rigorously with irrationality, unconscious motivation, and the prompting of social interest?

That question has not yet been answered. We are in the position of the legendary Presbyterian minister who set out his sermon under numbered headings and who, on coming to number four, said, "And now, fourthly, we come to a great difficulty. Let us look it firmly in the face and pass on. Fifthly, brethren . . ." I am not sure that Weber, despite his wrestling with these difficulties, did much better. Nor, as I am hoping to show, am I sure that these difficulties, fundamental though they appear, are either so important or so troublesome as Weber and his expositors and critics have believed. It is almost certainly not an illusion to believe that the bulk of the best and most original work in the physical and social sciences has been done by people who were either untroubled by problems of the foundation and method-ological justification of their subject, or who turned only to such questions once their early passion for the specific and urgent in their subject had been slaked. No doubt such comforting counsel is very Philistine, but it is unjust to assume that Philistines are always wrong.

What in fact saved Weber from drowning in a sea of intellectual and moral relativism was his passion for empirical knowledge. No one has ever accused him of lacking learning, and I know distinguished contempo-rary scholars who still read Weber precisely for the in-formation which he makes accessible on such a wide range of subjects. Yet his historicism and perhaps his nationalism did cut him off from researches that would have proved useful and corrective in his work and from an approach that would, at the least, have enabled him to order it better. I don't want to suggest that Weber should have read more, but that it would have been better for him if he had read differently.

Despite the thick volumes of comparative ethnology which were produced in Germany, the Germans made a comparatively small contribution to what is now called social anthropology—what we may take here as being the sociology of contemporary primitive peoples. The best work in this field in Weber's day was British, French, and American. No doubt the imperial successes of England and France and the territorial expansion of the United States at the expense of the Indians had something to do with this, but the Germans had great travelers, zealous missionaries, and something of an empire too. The Austrians, after all, can be thought of as having done better than the Germans in this field, and they entirely lacked two of these attributes. What is certain is that Weber was ignorant here and that the data of social anthropology would have simplified, corrected, and altered his work. What is more, Weber was negligent in his attention to a great predecessor and a greater contemporary.

I refer to Herbert Spencer and Emile Durkheim, both of whom availed themselves of the new data of anthropology. Spencer was an evolutionist, not a historicist—that, indeed, is his weakness—but his analysis of society was based on certain timeless taxonomic principles: these are the concepts of social structure, of function, and of institution. Weber never got any of these clear. To him society is not overtly describable in terms of a structure of social relations which subserve certain ends —that is, have functions—and which are ordered by institutional patterns. Such a structure can be viewed in a number of different ways, as one of relations between individuals, or between groups, or between the roles people play in society. Now with Spencer these possible alternatives are not spelled out but implied in a fairly commonsense mixture. Durkheim in his analysis of the forms of social solidarity was to do rather better. One of the influences on Durkheim was Weber's contemporary, Wilhelm Wundt. But Weber did not learn ahistorical (synchronic is a fashionable term) thinking from Wundt either. The richness of Weber is paid for in his exclusive historicism and a failure, which is not just one of clarity but of understanding, to grasp the direction of the main line of sociological thought. Given the existence of Wundt one cannot ascribe this entirely to the understandable autarchy of late-nineteenth-century German scholarship. Ideally, the sociologist should be a spectator and critic of the flux of time, not submerged in it or even—like the historians—victoriously embattled with it. Durkheim was perhaps the first man to realize this possibility.

On the other hand, Weber drew on a rich and very largely German store of knowledge and ideas which was not used on any scale by his great contemporaries. This was the history of religious and critical theology. The primary works in this field were concerned with Judaism and Christianity, but its range was that of all that we now call "the world religions," plus the religious systems of classical Greece and Rome. Here Weber read widely—British writers on Indian religion, Robertson Smith on the cults of the ancient Semites, a vast profusion of international studies of Confucianism and Taoism, and so on, as well as English and American sectarians, sources which are partly explicable in terms of his mother's highly personal form of late Calvinism. About religion, in a great age of scholarship, he is not parochial, although again one can feel it a pity that his knowledge of the best contemporary anthropological work was not greater. Had it been more extensive he might not only have concerned himself with the role of religion in the values whereby men act but also have seen that the fundamental categories of our understanding, so often bound up with our conception of the sacred, are implicated in social structure. But in an area where he achieved so much there is perhaps something petty in such a comment.

Ultimately the fact is that no general sociologist can ever of himself know quite enough, even if he is a demon-driven polymath. In Weber's time and place there was only emerging a community of sociologists with at once a division of labor and common interests and standards. The institutionalization of sociology was something to which Weber contributed by both his activity and his example. By doing so he helped to make of sociology that major form of our self-consciousness as social beings which it has become.

In all this I have been writing as though sociology had no quantitative aspect, as though, indeed, there was nothing to the popular image of the sociologist as someone who simultaneously pries into the affairs of his neighbors and yet is distanced from them by subjecting them to surveys and questionnaires that are then further removed from the untidy reality of affairs by being processed—preferably by computer. Of course, Weber had no computer—though the Austrian Herman Hollerith had invented his data-sorting machine in 1894. Yet by Weber's time survey research had had a long history and was well established, even though the use of sampling—an old tradition—only became formalized by such people as Bowley in the early twentieth century. Weber was well aware of these possibilities, but such studies contributed little to his major work and his contribution to them is not important.

Certainly he did produce early studies of agricultural laborers in east Prussia. And in 1907 Weber, under the influences of his brother the cultural sociologist Alfred

Weber, attempted a study of the effects of industrial life on the workers in large firms. He continued to be interested in questions of industrial sociology, workers' attitudes, and industrial psychology, and he also planned an abortive empirical research into the press and its effects. But only the early studies for the Social Political Union and the Evangelical Social Union seem to me of any interest today. However, Weber certainly knew what was going on in the world of social surveys and statistics. As we shall see, the one element of real value that he took from it is what we might call his "probabilistic" outlook.

The Pillars of Judgment

vi

Weber claimed that his intellectual milieu was dominated by Marx and Nietzsche, and that one could judge the members of that milieu very largely by the stand they took in relation to these towering personalities, so that anyone "who does not confess that he could not do the most important part of his own work without these two deceives himself and others." The role of Nietzsche in Weber's development and position, particularly in his later years, has become a dominant theme in modern Weber scholarship. As for Marx, one of the most frequently recurrent questions set students of sociology in Britain and America is a request to discuss the proposition that "Weber's sociology is a debate with the ghost of Karl Marx." What does all this amount to?

Nietzsche is the prophet of will, war, and power who shuddered at their actualization in his Germany, made, so he believed, coarse and stupid by power and the rise of the masses. Civilization, he argued, was undergoing a *Vermassung* and consequently a destruction of finesse, critical judgment, creative joy, and aristocratic values. Education hastened this process by going over to bourgeois, Philistine, and military goals of profit, rational efficiency, merely technical and banausic training. According to Gustav Stolper, Weber said in his seminar in Munich shortly before his death, "I have no political plans except to concentrate all my intellectual strength on one problem, how to get once more for Germany a great General Staff."[1] If Weber did actually say this, then I take it as an example of exactly what Nietzsche most deplored. But Nietzsche is never merely single-minded, and in this he was like Weber, only with greater strength and in a more extreme position: no one more than Nietzsche warned what the twentieth century could hold of horror and vulgar tyranny; no one more than Nietzsche lent the highest powers of mind and expression to ideas on which that tyranny could feed.

To Nietzsche the world had gone wrong through too much Christian virtue; it was corrupted by an excess of charity and mercy, and deceived by the false Christian assertion of an order in things other and better than that which we directly experience. Weber, ambiguous in attitude to his mother's faith and his father's easy materialism, must have found this tempting. We know

[1] G. Stolper, *This Age of Fable* (New York: Harcourt, Brace, 1942), p. 318*n*. I give this reference for, if true, it deserves record; if untrue, refutation.

that Weber's language often caused a scandalous reaction by its brutality and cynicism—something, I suspect, like that *Potsdamer Ton* adopted by the servants of the Empire, a tone of speech at once aristocratic and demotic, but always an assault on those to whom it was addressed in its assumption that the world was merely a barrack square. This rejection of the language of human consideration by a man who at other times impressed all who heard him by the beauty of his finely shaped sentences is, I think, a sympton of Nietzscheism at a lower level.

But was Weber greatly influenced by Nietzsche, or did he merely discover in Nietzsche a corroboration of his own divided, unresolved attitudes? I think the latter. Take the questions of "will" and the "struggle between values." Weber, accurately, I believe, held that values do not form a single, unambiguous hierarchy, and that no decision, save by consistent individual choice, is possible between competing values. Now of course most people do not bother to try to attain to a consistent position about values. On the contrary, they swim in a sea of contradictions, but they can achieve self-direction by the assumption that others will act in ways that can be predicted with probability, and that goals can be attained by rationally calculating and exploiting such probabilities. This type of behavior is universal: our civilization in particular has developed it into a dominant mode of conduct and of science. In contrast to this, one might set Nietzsche's ethic, whereby the superior man—the duty of the inferior is to surrender his will to that of the superior man; a dangerous counsel—shall choose, resolve, and act at hazard, gambling with death.

Now Weber does posit an opposite ethic to that of the national calculation of probabilities and a daily ethic of compromise. It is not, however, Nietzsche's in that it contains variety. Nietzsche's superior man chooses and maintains his choice in terms of the "will to power," whereas Weber recognizes as socially given a whole range of such choices, of such willed life-styles. Those committed to the life of aesthetic or religious values, who pursue honor or abstract duty, are careless of consequences in their commitment; but they have chosen, and to attain their ends of virtue they behave rationally enough. Their behavior is "value-rational" (*wertrational*) as opposed to a purposeful, judicious rationality (*Zweckrationales Handeln*). Thus Weber is in agreement with Nietzsche's attitudes of contempt, but not with Nietzsche's affirmation; that affirmation is but one path, and Weber's pluralism allows him a typical ambiguity.

It may not seem very positive or striking in our time to say that values are not in harmony with each other, that the true may be ugly, the holy repulsive, the beautiful feigning, and the good terrible. But in the nineteenth century, even in intellectual circles, it was moderately shocking; and to the traditions and faiths of his mother and his wife it was revolutionary and alienating —an explanation, possibly, of the hagiographic falsification which his wife employed in her biography of Weber. To find that science could neither order nor guarantee values was also surprising to both positivists and idealists. Nietzsche and Weber represent a reaction against those assumptions, a reaction, however, that would have seemed in its defiant tone a little excessive to sophisticated Britons who had read their Hume or

Frenchmen who had read their Baudelaire. It might also have seemed excessive to men less sheltered than Weber from the everyday deprivations and perils of life outside his privileged world.

The master of that underprivileged world, so his followers claimed, was Karl Marx. In the 1970s when at least a quarter of the world's population lives under regimes which are formally Marxist, and when to criticize Marxism even in the countries of Western Europe and North America is often taken as a proof of ignorance, paranoia, or corruption, it is important to remember three things about Weber's age. Marxism was not then a politically dominant creed. Neither was social thought, Left and Right, permeated by Marxist assumptions, nor was political thought shaped by its present polarities. Nor was the Marx known to that age the Marx of the late twentieth century, either in the vulgar image of Marx as prophet, legislator, and Newton of the social sciences, or in the polymorphous perverse figure, the infinitely slippery trickster of the mind who only seriously became an object of intellectual consciousness in the 1950s. Weber knew not Stalin, Mao, or Fidel; he did know the young Lukács, but the Lukács who sat at Weber's feet was caught up in the conflict of values, the concepts of virtue, beauty, and a romantic Slavophilism which reminds one of Rilke's claim that "Russia is a country bounded by God." He was concerned with Tolstoi, Prince Mishkin, Alyosha, rather than with Hegel and the young Marx. And Weber also knew something of the unfinished story of German social democracy.

The real founder of the German Social Democratic Party was Ferdinand Lassalle, but its ideology was for-

mally Marxist. This involved certain practical difficulties. For more than thirty years Marx was a testy
middle-aged gentleman—the noun is used accurately—
in London. Lassalle was on the whole rather a fine
figure, realistic but not base in his politics, romantic in
his life. But his party was saddled with Marxism. This
involved a belief in apocalyptic revolution, a year
greater than 1793 in which the despised and rejected
of the earth would revenge their ancient wrongs and
establish the realm of distributive justice forever in society. The very condition of "les damnées de la terre," as
the International has it, was the pledge and the instrument of their triumph. Science and Marxism were identical: by science, historical and economic, it was
demonstrated that the future lay with the proletariat.
God did not reign in heaven, and religion was at best
the cry of the heartless world, at worst the opium of the
people. But history had replaced God, and history, too,
was prophecy; after the judgment of the revolution
would come a new heaven and a new earth. And it was
the working class, ever exploited, ever in struggle, that
was the chariot of history advancing through industrialization, through the brutalities of economic exploi-
tation, through the recurrent miseries of capitalist crisis
to the goal of a just society.

All this was the formal belief system of steelworkers
in the Ruhr, miners in Silesia, weavers, shoemakers,
and worthy men like August Bebel in his prison cell
taking advantage of the enforced leisure to read science, philosophy, and economics. They had wives and
families and small savings. They showed great organiza-
tional talents and built up a trade-union movement.
They survived the persecutions—perhaps even thrived

on them—of Bismarck's antisocialist laws which Weber half approved. They took advantage of Bismarck's social legislation which in the early 1880s put Germany ahead of the world in terms of industrial and social assurance. They built up the first mass party on the European continent, a party inevitably bureaucratic, machine-committed, and elite-ridden, but theirs. They were also the enduring soldiers of the Empire. When that Empire fell in military disaster on the Western Front their leaders, simple enough men, despised by intellectuals like Weber, found themselves confronting a reality before which their decency, their party cunning, their deference, and their ideology were all inadequate. It was through this party of Bebel and Kautsky that Weber perceived, as in a glass darkly, the figure of Marx. The contradiction between the social-democratic ideology, built on the dream of the apocalyptic revolution, and the Lassallean idea of the permeation and capture of the state by the processes of representative government became fully evident only in Weber's last years.

In his inaugural lecture at Freiburg in 1895, Weber declared that the workers were politically immature and incapable of effective power, even though they were certainly right in many of their aims and some of their claims—those recognized by the Evangelical Social Union. At any rate the imperial state was stronger than the Social Democratic Party and, even if that party triumphed, it would become the prisoner of the state and at the same time, by its insistence on planning, extend the realm of an overmighty bureaucracy. In 1918, indeed, Weber said his position was hardly to be distinguished from that of the Socialists, but when he accompanied the German delegates to receive the peace conditions laid down in Versailles he spoke of their new masters to Field Marshal Ludendorff in other terms: "Do you credit that I take this swinish state of affairs that we now have as democracy?"

Against this background we can, I think, better understand the postures in which Weber confronted Marx. Weber said of his most famous essay, *The Protestant Ethic and the Spirit of Capitalism*, that it was a factual refutation of the materialist conception of history. (This was published in 1904–1905, two years after the first version of a now neglected book, Sombart's *Der moderne Kapitalismus*, to which I shall return.) On a first reading, *The Protestant Ethic* is unambiguous: the movement to a capitalist society was primarily caused by the habits, attitudes, and beliefs of Protestantism, more specifically of Calvinism, most specifically of English Puritanism. Puritans worked hard in their callings and amassed treasures which the asceticism of their creed did not permit them to consume. Yet that creed did not allow them to let their treasure lie idle. As a result they invested, denied the flesh, and produced a new economic order. But this is not an "idealist" position, claiming that the world is what men's thoughts make of it, but a claim that ideas as well as economic motives are interests too. As Weber said in another famous essay, *The Social Psychology of the World Religions*, "Not ideas, but ideal *and* material interests, directly govern men's concepts" (my italics). Reinhard Bendix, perhaps the most learned of all commentators on Weber, goes further, correctly I believe, and says, "According to Weber, material without ideal interests are empty, but ideals without material interests are impotent." Despite Bendix's accuracy, Weber's position, for all his reservations, is essentially biased to the "ideal" position: ideas in their presence or through their absence are the main determinants of the social.

Indeed, a sound Weberian might say that the above is too strong, for Weber's formal position differs, I think, from the over-all impression made by his work. The formal position is, first, that we are concerned in social studies only to grasp individual action, although of course such actions have unintended social consequences; second, that any basically uni-causal explanation of all events in society must be false—this is in accord with the neo-Kantian teaching of Heinrich Rickert, which Weber adopted, and with his view that the historical sciences, including sociology, are essentially concerned with what is individually specific. It follows from this that while Marx as a teacher, as an undeniably great economic historian, and as a brilliant political analyst is someone to be learned from, yet he has to be learned from piecemeal, serving as a source of particular illuminations and valuable models to aid one's thinking about the social and historical worlds. But the formal Weber is not the only Weber: to repeat, the real Weber gives to men's concepts and values a paramount role in the drama of social life.

Furthermore, for Weber, Marx is imprecise as to what is and is not part of the economic realm. Economic behavior, to Weber, is behavior that is intended to acquire resources which are also desired by others by means excluding force and fraud. But noneconomic factors affect what is or is not defined as a "resource" in a specific social situation—for example, religious or magical appraisals of what is valuable. Again, purely economic factors can act as the parameters within which

noneconomic behavior is possible: the economy itself
is a limiting, though not determining influence on society. Marx's simple economic materialism, Weber believes, dissolves under such considerations. Nor does
Marx's lumping of technics into "the means of production" satisfy him: Weber is surely correct in believing
that with any state of technology many economic
orders are possible; with any economic order many
technologies are compatible.

It is this that leads to a real insight: that there is a
problem as to why it was specifically western Europe
that uniquely created industrial capitalism, with its still
unmeasured consequences as a new kind of society.
Marx in a sense gives an answer to this in the first
volume of *Capital*, finding it largely but not exclusively
in the unique dynamics of the English agrarian system
in the age of the Tudors. But Marx does not ask the
negative question, why not elsewhere? Why not China,
Rome, India, or Peru? Weber does attempt this, and he
gives an unambiguous reply. This is in truth not to
debate with the ghost of Marx, but it is to be more per-
ceptive in a matter of importance not only for historians and sociologists but also for those who, however
rashly, would transform contemporary peasants into
industrial workers in an industrial milieu.

We may think that the debate between Marx and
Weber never really took place. We may hold, too, that
we know today, as Weber could not, a new Marx re-
vealed by scholarship and the publication of suppressed
or forgotten manuscripts. Whether this new Marx is
superior to the old is, however, another question, for
Marx may well have known exactly what he was about
when he discarded or withheld so much of his work

from publication. In the same way I would suggest that Weber's position in relation to Nietzsche is less interesting than is sometimes claimed. In his later years Weber doubtless found a new strength to express his feelings and attitudes through his reading of Nietzsche and his entry into circles in which Nietzsche's ideas were operative. But Weber did not derive his attitudes to the will, to values, or to aristocratic principles from Nietzsche; rather, he found corroboration for some of his positions in what he took to be Nietzsche's judgment on the world.

For Weber, Marx was a quarry of ideas and facts. This aspect of Marx—which by its piecemeal nature is remote from Marxism as theory or ideology—is often neglected. Marx was learned, ingenious, fertile of specific hypotheses, and as artful as a wagonload of monkeys. Weber's debt here is not one of generalized judgment, but it is considerable. So also is his obligation to his contemporary Sombart, whose learning and ingenuity about the nature of capitalist activity and its sources in war, luxury, and group psychology are today undervalued for reasons which derive less from Sombart's real defects than from the subsequent course of German history. (Weber's influence on Sombart is very great, but that is another story.) But it is the Marx of ideology, prophecy, and German social democracy who counts as a major object of Weber's public political consciousness.

The Formal Sociology

vii

Although Nietzsche and Marx in their different ways were men concerned to judge and condemn, this did not prevent either from contributing to scholarship both directly and through their influence. Nietzsche's *Birth of Tragedy* may be as completely rejected by orthodox classicists as is the labor theory of value by non-Marxist economists. But classics all the same are intellectually different and richer because of Nietzsche, and our understanding of society and history is the starker for the famous study of the wageworker's day and the attempt to trace the story of capitalist farming in England in the first volume of *Capital*. But though this, and more, is true enough, what characterized these two men was their passionate judgment and their apocalyptic myths.

Now Weber, though a great maker of social my-
thology, was primarily a scholar. He was a learned
man, a researcher, a theorist, seeking to diagnose rather
than engage in prophetic judgment. Weber's effort was
to attain to a diagnosis, not a prognosis, of his society,
his time, and his country. All of his sociology, even
when it roams most widely, is concerned with this goal
of understanding as completely and clinically as
possible.

What can we understand? We can understand the
actions of other men—not precisely perhaps, not always certainly, and we can be deceived. Nevertheless,
human action is in some measure open to us if only
because we, too, are human. This is the first step of
Weber's sociology. The second is the identifying of the
basic unit of the social—what Weber himself calls the
"atom," a word which I think carried for him not the
contemporary understanding of atoms as complexes of
more fundamental particles which are oddly probabilistic, but an idea of ultimate irreducibility, of a tiny
impenetrable essence. This atomic unit of the social is
the single deliberate action of an individual directed to
affecting the behavior of one or more other persons. Such
an action is to be distinguished from merely idle, auto-
matic, or self-directed deeds by virtue of its having
"intentional reference." That phrase means merely
what I have already said: it is performed with the intention of altering the behavior of others. The intention
is its essence, and its success, failure, partial success, or
unintended results are secondary factors. Society is the
sum of unit social acts, but clearly society is not a chaos.
These acts fall into categories and can be combined

into structures. It is to Weber the task of his kind of sociology—he recognizes that it is not the only kind—to understand the categories and structures of social actions in their actual and historical manifestations.

As I have said, Weber's starting point is his conception of the social sciences as *historical* sciences. He is a historicist in the sense that to him all human reality is to be understood in the dimension of time and by the methods of the historian.[1] Gradually, Weber's sociology emancipates itself from history, but he is always a historicist, to whom all the categories and structures of social action are relatively impermanent even when, like the imperial Chinese bureaucracy which so fascinated him, they endured for two millennia. He always, as far as the logic of science and history is concerned, declared himself a disciple of Heinrich Rickert, to whom history was knowledge of what is unique, specific, and individual, as opposed to the knowledge afforded by the physical sciences, which was abstract, general, and capable of being stated in the form of invariable natural laws. Out of the chaos of past transactions we select for the purposes of history and the *human* sciences those which relate to human values.

The totality of real events, physical as well as historical, is not to be encapsulated by any science. We can never know with complete knowledge, for the world is too rich. Our systems of laws are not nature's but our own and are provisional; the task of making and amending them is never done. Sociology complements

[1] The word "historicism" has other, more recent meanings, but as an account of Weber this older usage is sufficient.

but does not transcend history in its attempt to grasp the structure of social behavior, nor can it replace the historian's concern with unique events and persons.

In his historical studies, Rickert gave to human values a central place. Outside the stream of temporal events, historians had stood, he claimed, confident in their objectivity, in that the value of truth provides at least one undoubted shared value. Rickert also held that even if all values other than truth are in doubt, no one can dispute that life and history present men with universal and problematic meanings and values. But in these arguments Weber tacitly went another way. This, I think, took him far from Rickert. For, as we saw, Weber found values manifest in conflict and irreducible to a transcendent order. He starts from his own valuations, or from the value-questions of his age. This is a form of relativism, but it is a relativism which is not complete, not without at least one rule. To Weber all history and every sociology is relative, but necessarily and properly so: the realm of values does not guarantee objectivity, but, having chosen his interest and thus asserted his value-position, the historian or sociologist is committed to such objectivity and truth as can, painfully, be attained. Every diagnosis involves, after all, standards and value-judgments as to the proper working of the patient.

Weber's patient is society. His principal diagnostic device is the "ideal type." An enormous volume of ink has been used in discussing what Weber really meant by this term. My own view is that the problem is very difficult but also, for any present-day sociology, quite trivial, and that just as one may be bemused by complex legerdemain and yet not seriously occupied by it, so one may regard the whole issue of "ideal types." But two things must be said to clear away understandable and recurrent errors. Weber did not mean that his ideal types were in some sense good or noble: "Ideal" here simply means "not actually exemplified in reality." No element of value is involved. Secondly, he did not intend his "ideal typical method" to invent any novel instrument of analysis. Rather, by this he meant to explain and refine what social scientists and historians actually do. The ideal type begins with making overt the tacit, actual methodology of other men, and by making this methodology publicly clear Weber hopes to improve the self-consciousness and rigor of the social sciences.

Why "ideal"? Plenty of things and people are typical: remarks like "He is a typical stockholder," "That is a typical cardiac lesion," "There is a typical Picasso," refer to a representative normality of experience. One might if one wished call such examples "real types." They can be social: "That is a typical contract" or "They have a typical marriage." But as we said, "ideal" in Weber's concept means "not actually exemplified in reality." So the ideal type is not an extreme "real type." If I say, "He is a typical stockbroker, indeed he is the stockbroker *in excelsis*," then I am still talking about actual things, if of extreme cases. This gets one a little closer to the ideal type, but not all the way. "Paganini is the perfect violinist" is an extreme case: he has all the qualities of a violinist, *and* I am claiming he has them to perfection. If I mean that perfectly seriously, then, so far as violin-playing is concerned, ideal and reality coincide. But of course they never do: I can always imagine some possible extension of skill or expression that would make Paganini even better. It is this imagination that is

the key: the ideal type is the pure case, never actualized, uncluttered by extraneous attributes and ambiguities.

In one way my example of Paganini is misleading in
that it makes one think by association of an ideal perfection and excellence. It must be remembered that for
Weber there is an ideal type of embezzlement, of any
crime, horror, or sin. When one uses such concepts as
"capitalist," "feudal," "entrepreneur," "romantic,"
"charismatic," and so on, one is, consciously or not,
using ideal types. All such complex descriptive and generalizing terms are ideal types in the social sciences.

But why are they not more, why are they not specifi-
cations of social reality? Here one comes back to the
slipperiness of Weber, his delight, as I think, in the
appearance of never being finally committed, of always
having the ace of ambiguity up his sleeve. (It is one
part of what the great historian Friedrich Meinecke
meant when he called Weber "the German Machia-
velli.") This slipperiness is not merely an attitude, but is
part of Weber's appraisal of the even greater slipperiness
of social reality and of how the Proteus of history may
be seized. To Weber, as we saw, society is made up of the
interplay of unit social acts so numerous, so kaleido-
scopic, that we can only seize and hold them in the
mind by some device such as the ideal type, knowing
all the time that the device is itself merely a tool, something we have made, not something we have found as a
constituent of the real. To be reminded of this is very
useful and often salutary. It is nothing more.

If I sit down to work out a model—as I would call it
—of a bureaucratic order, made up of certain elements
of hierarchical organization, specialization of function,

concentration of responsibility, rules of procedure, and so on, I do not say to myself that I am constructing (or analyzing) an ideal type. I know perfectly well what I am about, just as Monsieur Jourdain in Molière's *Le Bourgeois gentilhomme* knew exactly what he was saying, even though he was struck with wonder at being told he was speaking prose. The parallel is close: for the purposes of language study it is important to be able to at least tell most prose from most verse, but it is not of importance to a native-speaker ordering his supper to be distracted by reflection on the fact that he is not doing so in iambics. Methodology is, similarly, a distraction to science except under certain rare circumstances (which does not mean that methodology is not worthwhile in itself, to methodologists). But what of these "rare circumstances"? I do not mean by them the common scholarly activity of breaking up and reformulating someone else's system: that is one of the core activities of the knowledge industry. What I do mean is that in principle one can come up against instances where a model or a system of thought can no longer be saved for scientific respectability by any of the devices such as elaboration, the addition of a special theory, etc., which are commonly employed. Such cases have, I believe, occurred in physics during the last century. I can find no evidence of them in the history of the social sciences, but in principle they are possible and even, I would guess, probable. Then we may want to use Weber's full battery of devices and employ all his ambiguous ingenuity. Otherwise we may rest with our rough, in part always unexamined, models of social behavior. Rather than with a strict "ideal typical" method.

Weber's great, unfinished, posthumously published book *Economy and Society* (*Wirtschaft und Gesellschaft*) begins as though everything in sociology had to be created *de novo*, out of chaos. This exercise of definition and analysis is complex, powerful, daunting, and often exemplary. But of course Weber knew very well that the subjects with which he was concerned had a long genealogy and he accepted much of the vocabulary of previous scholars and his contemporaries —even of those contemporaries with whom he most disputed. His lexicon of concepts consisted of items taken from law, history, economics, and philosophy. This lexicon provided the foundations of his attempt to reconstruct society by advancing a number of models which would enable society as it concerned and interested him to be diagnosed, even if not into a single comprehensible scientific model. This meant that Weber had to have some kind of working classification of the various major forms of social action. One way to that classification would have been by the kind of institutional study carried out by his English contemporary, Leonard Hobhouse. But this was not Weber's way. With Hobhouse he shared a concern with rationality, but Weber was to attack directly, not by way of institutions. He attempted to classify all acts under four heads, complexly related.

An act, to Weber, is rational when it can be described as being in accord with the canons of logic, the procedures of science or of successful economic behavior— that is to say, when it is end-attaining in its intentions and in full accord with factual knowledge and theoretical understanding in its means. Where the choice of an end from among other ends and the choice of means satisfies these criteria, an act is fully rational. On the other hand, where the ends are given by values—religious, moral, or aesthetic—or where such values affect the choice of means, then we have behavior classified as "value-rational." However, if the ends of an act are accepted for reasons of tradition—a kind of value—and the means, which need not thereby be ineffective, are given also by tradition in whole or part, we have behavior of a kind that has been the dominant mode in most societies of most ages. Finally, according to Weber, acts may be merely moved by the affections and passions—"affectual action." This kind of behavior is, when the end and the means are both derived from the emotions, at the opposite pole in Weber's system from the calculatingly rational deed.

Now Weber is not completely consistent throughout his work in his use of these categories. What is more, if we use ends and means as subcategories of behavior, a wide variety of forms—at least ten—of behaviors is comprehended. How are these empty, classificatory boxes to be filled? And where does the concept of "charisma" which we met at the outset fit in? To answer these points we will have to become more concrete, but before that we must look at another set of Weber's categories, a set which is concerned with the central practical interests, public and private, of his life. What is the basis of political obligation, of our uncoerced obedience to the state? Traditionally, this is the central problem of British and French political philosophy. In imperial Germany the question could be answered by many routes, given that history of varied elements and that constitution of heterogeneous claims and institutions. Not one of these was clearly adequate.

For what constitutes the *legitimacy* of power? To what secular authority should a man bow? Weber argues that power which is regarded as legitimate by the obedient ceases to be naked power or coercion and becomes authority by three paths: these are the traditional, the rational-legal, and the charismatic.

According to the traditional path, time makes good; we have always done things in such a way and obeyed people of such a family or holders of such an office who have got into the office by a recognized quality of holiness or valor or merit: these are the forms of traditional authority. There is a wisdom in old things and the *mos maiorum*. But why should time legitimate? It is not obvious, and I believe that it is thought to do so only where the past is felt to have at one time been sacred, being endowed with a holy quality that can be explained by reference to the actions of the gods, or an accord with a partially or wholly lost age of virtue, or a semidivine establishment of families or institutions. Both those who command and those who obey must accept these beliefs and feelings.

As regards the rational-legal path, reason is being; reason is science, is technical, is law: these are the foundations of rational-legal authority. In this case, the legitimacy is that of a unique efficiency. Rational-legal authority is supremely good at the attainment of ends. I believe that here, too, there is much of the sacred, although in a special form; for there does exist the faith in certain industrial societies that science, and scientific procedures, and procedures that mimic what are believed to be the forms of science, are imbued with the idea of the holy. This is not, of course, the whole story —though such a faith was very typical of the Hohenzollern empire in the heroic age of German science and industrialization, just as it is prevalent today, especially in Communist countries. However that may be, Weber is not concerned with this possibility. The legal-rational is, to him, what it claims to be: what he questions and deplores are its consequences.

According to Weber's final argument divine grace is self-guaranteeing, and disobedience to it is blasphemy; here is the claim of the charismatic leader or prophet: God cannot be other than the ultimate legitimacy. (For God, where necessary, read *the class, the people, the folk, the march of history, inevitable destiny*, and so on: secular idolatry is still the worship of images.) Charisma is neither long enduring nor extensible very far. Those who accept the charismatic authority of their leader do so as a chosen band. The demands of everyday life for order, continuity, and predictability cannot be reconciled with a constant eruption of divine inspiration. Charisma, then, becomes routinized in ritual, administration, and discipline.

Coercive power seeks legitimacy for itself, and even those who are coerced by it tend to try to find some legitimacy in their fate and thus in their rulers. There is a quest to accept, to find or invent legitimacy as part of a general quest which Weber seems to think a universal human characteristic. Human life seeks meaning: society is made possible, however precariously, by meaning and value or that search for them which is itself an embodiment of meaning—since no quest can be undertaken without a conviction, however doubting, that the intention and the goal are worthwhile.

Thus in a sense Weber's end is his beginning. We are back with the unavoidability of valuation, of choice where there is incompatibility and contradiction and no transcendent order. The world of man in society is a world of unit social acts, ordered by the need to make choices for an always uncertain future in terms of some principle of choice which we call a value. It has been objected that existence and value-choice cannot be conceptually separated from each other: I do not see that this is a criticism of Weber, but rather an affirmation of his position.

Weber the sociologist was, indeed, an existentialist *avant la lettre*. This claim has little to do with Weber's relationship to Nietzsche and nothing to do with his encounter with Kierkegaard under the influence of the young Lukács. Nevertheless, I think the term "existentialist" is precisely accurate as a description of what lies at the heart of Weber's theory of society.

But if that is so, Weber in his personal life and in his deployment of his sociology as an expression of his own being is a very odd existentialist. Again and again we find him resisting commitment and engagement and welcoming ambiguity or indecision. Yet even then he goes no further, undertaking neither the Pyrrhonism nor the poetic insight into the metaphorical nature of all discourse which are the justifications of irony. Thus he was, I suppose, an existentialist constantly guilty of bad faith. Some, of course, would call his form of bad faith scientific integrity.

It is certainly very human. Weber practiced at least one part of what he preached. This world of ours is, just because it is human, in principle open to human understanding. We are not limited, as with nature, to a search for laws, but we can—making use of such sociological "laws" as we can discover—hope to go further and know the causal and motivational nexus which yields a specific social situation. Such a situation may well be a very foreign one from a remote culture, but it cannot but be humanly accessible. Thus Weber tacitly accepts a psychic unity of humankind. Weber's strongest claim to sociological greatness, I suppose, comes here, in that, alone of the great sociologists of his age, he faced the fullness of history and attempted to bring to it human sympathy and humane imagination to serve as the foundations of sociological method. Of course, in his actual practice he was limited by his own human capacities.

The Substantive Sociology

●　●　●

VIII

Society is problematic because we cannot fore-know all the consequences—or for that matter all the determinants—of our acts. Act as we may with a maximum of calculated rationality, based on a careful assessment of empirically tested evidence, we still act with others, and the results of our deeds, even if we attain our purposes, are not exhausted by our goals. No one sat down in the centuries that followed the decline of the Carolingian Empire and decided to establish that order which we call feudalism, first in northern France, thereafter in England, Sicily, the Latin Kingdom of Jerusalem, and elsewhere. Rather, that regime emerged out of the desire for power and the need for order, the tenacity of possession and the obedience of prudence, of innumerable people. No one intends to establish a market economy: such a state of affairs comes into being through the individual bargaining arrangements of people exchanging goods or services to maximize their advantages or minimize their deprivations. And so on: the Anglo-Dutchman Bernard Mandeville saw how "private vices" by their demands on the economy could prove to be "public benefits." To that most perfect social scientist Adam Smith the allocation of resources that results from the interactions of the market produced a result in concordance with what would be the fiat of a supremely calculating force of reason. But there was no such force. It was as though some "invisible hand" was at work, the godlike hand of an omnipotent accountant. In Germany, Kant called such enormous unintended consequences the "heteronomy of ends." We work more than we can mean or know.

Feudalism, and the capitalism of a free market economy, are ideal types. Even in the England of William the Conqueror or the Antioch of Bohemund feudalism as a model was not perfectly exemplified. Even in England between 1846 and 1871 a free market capitalist economy of the type that economists described and, increasingly, prescribed was not to be found. (Neither was the case stronger in late nineteenth-century America, with its state intervention to aid those who grasped for economic power, or in imperial Germany, where the state was a part of the economic order, intervening both in the labor market in the interests of domestic harmony, and also in the pattern of finance and industry in the interests of national might.) Now Weber would certainly have disapproved of the phrase I am going to use, for it commits sins against the merely heuristic intent which he professed and against his nominalism, but I believe it accurately describes what his substantive work is concerned to do: that concern was to put flesh on the bony skeleton of the ideal types, choosing those particular ideal types which demonstrate the trickster quality in society, that is, which are abstractions of those phenomena which exemplify the heteronomy of ends.

In his early, enormously detailed studies of the conditions of the rural workers east of the Elbe—studies essentially without an upshot, although directed to questions of practical policy—Weber is dealing with the consequences of economic rationality. Semi-servile strata for the workers involve also social obligations for the masters. In the east of the Empire, where the expansion of the Teutonic Knights, Electors of Brandenburg, and Frederick the Great had resulted in Junker rule over a partly alien, Polish-speaking, and Catholic underclass, economic rationality—that is, the desire to maximize profits—was weakening the German nature of the region. Immigrant Slavs were coming into a society always in part colonial. They were a rural proletariat, whose only social relations with the rulers were economic. The bonds of servility and obligation no longer held. Workers in principle might become tenant farmers, but they were psychologically "proletarianized." They demanded more cash. They could not compete economically with the culturally inferior Slavs[1]—yet it

[1] Weber was not a racialist. He believed, however, in an inherent superiority in Germany which can be called cultural at best, mystical at worst. In his latter years, certain Russians such as Tolstoi and Soloviëv came to mean much to him intellectually, but he never seems to have really considered Poles or Russians at large as good as his fellow countrymen —as peoples with equal rights to their own inspirations or with equal, if different, virtues and qualities.

was in the cash interest of landlords to employ these Slavs. The Junkers, the heart of Prussian power, fiercely loyal in politics, were yet in the economic sphere a menace to the security of the eastern marches. The Slavs were not just a threat to patriarchal relations and old solidarities but also a symptom of the clash between an old Germany and a new, between the interests of the economy and the maintenance of Germany as a "power state." And none of this had been consciously willed.

Weber is par excellence the sociologist of the economic order. He does not confuse economics with sociology, but he believes that the sociologist must be concerned with purely economic institutions, such as stock markets, just because they are institutions and are thus societal objects. Also, the sociologist has to be aware that major social formations—paramountly those of religion and of the family—have economic consequences. These consequences are in turn limiting factors—even at times determinants—of the social situation. Economic resources and arrangements condition social interests. But the resulting sociology of the economic order is elaborate, confusing and confused. If Weber had lived, he might have refined it, but I doubt this. The elaboration and muddle are as present in the early studies of the rural workers in the east as they are painstakingly made manifest in the incomplete *Economy and Society*.

What Weber is trying to do is nothing less than to comprehend capitalism as a civilization, the civilization of the modern western world. To him, capitalistic activity is all but a universal feature of human societies. Viking raiders and the priestly treasurers of archaic divine kingdoms, for example, are engaged in capitalistic action. But capitalism itself is historically extremely concrete. To understand even the petty issues of farming in eastern Germany, one must understand the uniqueness of capitalism as a western system, historically specific. In the lectures published after his death as *General Economic History*, Weber gives a formal specification of capitalism: it is present "wherever the industrial provision for the needs of a human group is carried out by the methods of enterprise, irrespective of what [particular] need is involved. More specifically, a rational capitalistic establishment is one with capital accounting, that is, an establishment which determines its income-yielding power by calculation according to the methods of modern bookkeeping and the striking of a balance."

Capitalism then is not merely western but comparatively modern. Weber ascribes the accountant's balance sheet to the Dutchman Simon Stevin—and in my edition of Weber gets Stevin's dates a century late—but in fact double-entry accounting and the balance sheet are pre-Reformation Italian devices. But Weber does give the recent fact of capitalism very ancient origins in western society. The tendency to an increasing component of rational action in society as against traditional modes begins in ancient Greece, and the invention of coined money by the Greeks is an illustration of this fact, for money makes quantitative economic rationality easily possible as a common measure both of things and of abstractions such as "work" and "risk." Disciplined armies are highly rational means to ends; so is religious discipline which, at its peak in western monasticism, orders men to their eternal goal. To Weber there is in all rationality a component of deprivation: the soldier is deprived of his spontaneous and reflecting being (the Prussian Army was based on a complete automatism of ordered obedience which Weber both approved of and deplored) and the monk too is not just an ascetic (that is true of all hermits and of the monasticism of the Thebaid), but a disciplined ascetic. Disciplined deprivation is in Weber's thought an essential aspect of rational action in the pursuit of its ends. The capitalist is the ascetic of economic gain. Capitalism is the manifestation of a spirit, a character: it is much more than a constellation of productive, exchange, and accounting devices.

It is worth remarking at this point that Weber is really very little interested in industrialism as such. In his treatment of the transformation of technology and organization which we call the industrial revolution, of the factory and factory labor, of the enormous and continuing transformation of productivity which distinguishes industrial societies from all previously existing modes of life and society, Weber is merely conventional and often cursory. Despite this, commentators have tried to make much of him as an industrial sociologist—we saw earlier his empirical interest in the attitudes and experiences of industrial labor—but it is impossible to see Weber as a major analyst in this area. His contemporaries Werner Sombart, J. A. Hobson, and Thorstein Veblen in Germany, England, and America are rich— particularly the latter two—where Weber is poor. It is this point, I think, that also renders so many of the comparisons of Marx with Weber pointless. Their concerns are too often not the same. Criticism of Marx, an instructive pursuit, is only in one sense valuably conducted by comparison with Weber, and that sense has nothing to do with the sociology of the industrial order.

But if we say that capitalism is its spirit, what do we mean? Capitalism to Weber is a huge historical movement in a specific geographical and cultural area, so polymorphous and perverse in its course and origins that all generalizations must fall unusually short of the reality. Thus one must weave a net in which to fish up this leviathan out of many interlinked ideal types, and one must use that net with caution and after long practice at the trawl. One can regard Weber's life as that practice and *Economy and Society* as the net. The use of the term "spirit" is then cautionary: its very vagueness is necessary where all is so tentative.

The above paragraph, I think, represents Weber and the pieties about this part of his work adequately, but it also does him less than justice in that he was too good a scholar and thinker to be always consistent. I am quite clear that he thought capitalism was the consequence of the actions of a limited number of men who possessed (or were possessed by) a common spirit which produced a complex of rational modes of profit-making— which complex is what we call "capitalism." With Weber we are to view this spirit and its unintended consequences from the top downward: capitalism is the work of capitalists, not the common experience of a special kind of society. Weber was to claim that he was not trying to explain the origin of capitalism by this spirit of the capitalists, but I don't think one can read him and also accept this recurrent point, typical of his ambiguously polemical style.

Posterity has not been wrong in its concentration on the long essay, or series of fragments, published in 1904–1905 as *The Protestant Ethic and the Spirit of*

Capitalism. It is extraordinarily interesting, and it carries with it the conviction, justly, that somewhere in the area of its concerns lies an important but not fully formed truth about society. To have read it is necessary for any understanding of our age. Weber starts off from the commonplace position of his time that Protestantism is correlated with predominant wealth and power in the form we know as capitalism. Is this accidental? We have seen that there were capitalistic activities before capitalism and in noncapitalist societies. There were also capitalists before the Reformation, but Weber disposes of them cavalierly enough as exceptional "supermen of economic rationality." But capitalism and the Reformation as major historical movements are too closely linked in time for any mere contingent play of events to be a probable account of what happened. Indeed, an examination of how theological positions, everyday ethics, and economic behavior run together forces us to conclude that there does exist some causality.

The theology on which Weber concentrates is Calvinism. But Calvin and Knox were not concerned to change traditional economic ethics, and their views triumphed both in areas like Holland, where capitalism was early manifest, and in Scotland and Geneva, where it developed fairly late. Even so, Weber extends the working of Calvinism to English and colonial American Puritanism and then to other forms of Protestantism. How just this extension, vital to Weber's case, may be we cannot pursue here. However, in Calvinism one has no confidence of election to salvation: all one can do is to have faith and reinforce that faith by diligent, self-denying labor in one's vocation. One can never relax, and unremitting strenuous work at one's trade and in life, prayer and worship are obligatory. (One can in fact find little basis for all this in Calvin's *Institutes* and contrary counsel in Knox, but I think Weber is correct enough in his picture of how Calvinism was actually understood.) Toil, to Puritan preachers, expelled evil, impure, pleasure-seeking, and sensual impulses. Time, God's greatest, briefest gift, must not be wasted. The fruits of toil might signify divine approval, if they were not enjoyed. As an everyday ethic, Weber argues, this theology led to the accumulation of capital. Its unintended consequence was capitalist society. Finally, the ethic could be and was separated from the theology and became an autonomous secular force, "adequate to modern capitalism in its formative time."

Weber hedges this account around with reservations. He hints more than he says. He insists that he is showing us only one side of the coin and that the other, the material interests and socioeconomic situation of Europe, is also there. But the drift is unmistakable. In this unique transformation of traditional Europe to capitalism, what people thought and believed was decisive. This thesis is borne out in two ways: elsewhere, for example in his justly famous essay on the sociology of the city and in his lectures on economic history, Weber does turn the coin over. But so far as novel suggestions about the sources of capitalism are concerned he has very little to tell us. Secondly, Weber was to write a great deal more about religion in society. One of the core things in these writings is the demonstration that the creeds and establishments of non-European faiths,

lacking the drive and burden of anything like a Protestant ethic, did not lead even advanced and complex
societies into the rational order of capitalism.

What Weber is concerned with in the sociology of
religion is of course not religion in itself, its truth or
falsity, nor is it the elaboration of a general theory, like
Durkheim's, of the function of the religious in the
social: it is the working of religion on everyday life, on
political, administrative, economic, and moral behavior
in different historical situations that he tries to understand and reduce to order.[2] The process of understanding means that the sociologist must put himself in a
curious position of suspense between a universal skepticism and an equally universal acceptance of thought-
worlds other than his own. This suspense is a source
both of tension and, to those who enjoy the spectator's
ambiguous role, of pleasure. But the task itself is, I
think, misconceived: the varieties of religious expression in the banality of common life is too great, too
much studied, for an approach that is neither Durk-
heimian nor Spencerian to succeed.

Primarily, there are two alternative religious modes.
(It must be remembered that Weber was no ethnolo-
gist, even of the armchair.) There are those religions
which adapt men to the world, making tolerable by law
and ritual the disorder of experience, and the religions
of salvation which accept the disorders and perils of
being with resignation, repudiate the pleasures of the
world, and seek a transcendent other-worldly goal. In
his study of Confucianism and Taoism (translated mis-

[2] Hence Weber's sociology of religion is of a piece with all
his sociology.

leadingly under the title *The Religion of China*), Weber finds the best exemplification of a religion that is this-worldly, concerned with the right conduct—that is, the ritual conduct, of men here and now—in Confucianism. Ethics are bureaucratized; laws are legitimated by being sacred; but the sacred thing about them is the letter, not the spirit. In fact, emperors and priests might be better served not by such formal laws but by more personal justice; however, the interest groups on whom they rely press them into this ritual, subtle formalism. Traditional Judaism in the nonprophetic age belongs to the same species as Confucianism, but as the religion of a minority it has a double code—inward and strong, outward and more permissive. In such religions the problematic nature of being is lost sight of; meaning is devalued, practice elevated. Priests are functional officeholders and teachers of right conduct.

By contrast, the religions of salvation turn on issues of meaning; charismatic leaders emerge in them and prophecy is one of their modes. Time does not so much legitimate them as, often by way of tribulation, it redeems. It can redeem by works of virtue or of observance—to Weber, in this context, that means a rejection of rationality—or of participation through ecstasy, mystical or orgiastic, in the other-worldly divine nature. Such faiths have stored in them revolutionary and unpredictable potential.

When in the salvation religions there is present an actual savior figure, bridging the natural and nonnatural gulf, then believers move through society with a confidence at once somnambulistic and frighteningly autonomous. Invariably, the relation between salvation religions and their social structures is one of tension, and where salvation is mediated by a redeemer, then the tension is maximized: men desert their primordial bonds of kin and place; they question the economic order and its calculating rationality—even Confucianism opposed rational capitalistic behavior, not because it was in any way like a creed of salvation, but because its legitimacy was that of tradition—and they call in doubt the political hierarchy because it is a hierarchy and a denial of the brotherhood of the saved in which there are neither bond nor free. Salvation is individual but not local: all men may share, and its values are in principle universal, that is to say, socially unbounded. But, alas, societies *are* their boundaries, both internal and external.

As we saw, the gifts of the spirit become routinized. Compromise, institutionalization, and bureaucracy supervene. Religions become dogmatic and learned, and hence new tension develops, whereby this learning in its turn comes into conflict with the even more rationalistic learning of the secular order, of philosophy, scholarship, and positive science. Nor is religious learning a food for the soul hungry for salvation. Routinized and learned, caught in a double bind with the secular order and the demands of faith, charisma and new beginnings intervene. The cycle—though Weber does not call it that—resumes in a new form. There is in religion a war and a succession of three ideal types: the magician, the priest, and the prophet. More deadly still is the war of all three with the secularized man of learning, suspending belief in the interest of rational understanding. This war Weber does not so much examine as exemplify.

This growth of the rational component of behavior is

also to be found, according to Weber, in the history of law, which begins in charisma and religion, separates and secularizes out of this origin, and becomes a source of tension for the religions of ritual order and, more strongly, salvation. Law as lawyer's law, rationally instrumental, is an index of the growth of secularization. Together with economic rationality it is the nemesis of an order of meaning in which society is in touch with and bound to the sacred. In such a writer as Kant we find ethical rationality as a prescription in its most extreme and most demanding form, confronting men with duties unmediated by emotion or tradition, which, when embodied in jurisprudence, imposes a tyranny of reason on the weak and human too great to be endured for long.

Justice in ceasing to be divine becomes necessary. I do not mean by that a practical necessity, but a necessity ascribed to things. Reason as sovereign over action justifies all instrumentalities of behavior and all the consequent conditions of men. A rational market economy is in this sense just. Those who are disadvantaged by it are made lowly by necessity in accord with reason. To Weber, class—as distinct from Indian castes or the feudal social estates—is a reflection in society of the working of the quantitative rationality of the market. It is manifest by who gets what and who does what in capitalist society: what people get and do does not consist only in income, capital, and work, but in "life chances." These are the expectations, probabilistically estimable, of length and quality of life. Social status is a function of the general estimation of life chances as good or ill, as invidious or as conferring prestige in the rationality, the highest of all rationalities, of capitalism.

There is, however, no reason to expect the lowly to like this: on the contrary, one must expect them to struggle above all by instrumental politics against a society thus ordered. But in a world of so many factors and considerations should one wish them to succeed? As we know, Weber answered that ambiguously. And can they succeed? I do not believe that Weber thought that they could do more than win an alleviation of their position by rational political and economic organization.

Thus we are left with one possibility, that of a charismatic politics of the masses making all things new: in what shape of promise or of terror Weber could not tell.

The Diagnosis of Our Time

•

ix

The English sociologist Hobhouse, at much the same time as Weber, worked with comparable learning on a greater range of data concerning the values and the faiths of men. One of his principles was that there is a secular tendency for the role of reason to increase, despite reversals or divagations, in human affairs. Reason, to Hobhouse, confronted and comprehended the irrational in action but was not tainted by it. Reason teased out the constituents of actual situations and the value-problems associated with them. Reason thus resolved conflicts and brought an increasing, if never perfect harmony to human affairs. In many of the specific analyses, Hobhouse's *Morals in Evolution* and *Social Development* are superior to what Weber has to say at corresponding points (see, for example, the great chapter on justice and law in the earlier book). Like Weber, Hobhouse flirted with the political and learned from his experiences as a leader writer on *The Manchester Guardian* under C. P. Scott, its most famous editor, and with the trade unions. He had the enormous advantage over Weber of understanding what had been established about the structure and function of social institutions from Ferguson to Spencer. But, unlike Weber, he was not driven by demons and terrors, nor was he sophisticated by being shy and ambiguous. As a result he has left us no diagnosis of his time to reverberate in the minds of men in our later age.

Weber formally evades any scheme of stages of social development or any system of historical cycles, and yet it is impossible not to find in him both such a scheme and a kind of recurrent cycle. The advantage of rational action is gaining advantage: it is in the business of trying to attain ends, the most effective of the devices produced by the historical experience of mankind. Thus it gradually tends to supplant all other modes of social action. The concept of positive science, deliberate technical innovation, uniform rational social control and law, dispassionate and impersonal administration, and calculated economic action are all historical products characteristic, in their developed forms, of European civilization. These forms were bought at the price of the deprivations and individual burdens of Protestantism. Where the religious order avoided these specific asceticisms and demands, then the most rational of all social systems, advanced capitalism, did not emerge. (To Weber, "rational" is a value-word, although he does not equate "rational" with "good.") There is in all societies a tendency toward an increasing component of rationality in social life, but only in our societies is this movement fully actualized. This tendency involves the displacement from life of the emotional and the traditional modes of legitimate behavior as socially unacceptable. As a result the world loses its savor. The spontaneous affections of the heart, the hatreds of the moment, the comely and honorable ways of tradition are all forbidden. Reason illuminates all being with a shadowless and clinical light before which fly poetry, faith, and myth. One does not even find in the merciless light of reason the consolation of injustice: reason is its own justification, the legitimator of its own necessities.

Weber took from the poet Schiller a phrase that is usually translated as "the disenchantment of the world." The German, in fact, means something more precise: the driving out of magic from things. The Magus Weber is the last magician, a Prospero who must bury his staff under the gray sky of everyday rationality. He was himself an unspecialized man: the world of reason is a world in which men lose their manifold natures in the specialized division of labor, devoting themselves to unambiguously defined tasks. Weber's life was a struggle against such a destiny—the destiny of the bureaucrat, the officeholder in big government or big business or big political parties. It is, he wrote, "the dictatorship of the officials, not of the proletariat, that is marching on." He did not love this fact.

He found the orderly routine of a secularized world oppressive and calculating, and mechanical order crushing. Weber loved the power of the state that embodied these things and hated that state for embodying them. He loved that freedom, which he understood as the liberty of the educationally privileged and economically secure, that is, as the precarious product of inegalitarian society in its historical movement. People will always be in tension with the social roles that society requires them to play; and freedom is the rare consequence for a few when that tension accidentally is relaxed. Objectively, in a world of rationality, of bureaucracy, and of the masses, one should not expect its survival. Indeed, we should expect disenchantment to become complete, bureaucracy and regulation to be universal, and secularization to displace all the meanings of faith and hope while administrative welfare eliminates charity.

But, after all, this scheme of development is itself but another ideal type. And there is in history a lesson of a cyclical kind. When the world is overroutinized, over-bureaucratized, then the prophets and the Caesars return, dowered with charisma. But is that a hope? As I said at the end of Chapter viii, Weber did not know and never loved Caesars. His own constitution-mongering in his last days, as the Weimar Republic came painfully to birth, is not very impressive and is caught between an ingenuity about electoral and constitutional arrangements and the wariness of the Magus who knows that all his spells will lose their power if he finally commits himself as a participant in the struggles of value in the arena of politics. It is in this diagnosis that the secret of Weber's continued reputation most resides. Like all of him, it offers us tension, polarity, and ambiguity.

There is, however, another Weber, and that Weber is another matter. The American sociologist Talcott Parsons discovered Weber's work in the 1920s. From it he extracted and elaborated something latent, a systematic sociology of great range and power, although at the time I write not very fashionable. This system, carried by Parsons' energy and ability far beyond anything that Weber achieved and embodying other constituents from both the larger sociological tradition and from Parsons' own researches, is undoubtedly Weberian. It is at once an invention and a discovery. But it is not, I think, all there is in Weber: its very articulation and specificity which are its strengths (and which expose it, therefore, to attack) somehow deny the liquid and evasive richness that is the secret of Weber's strongest sorcery over all his successors.

In his last years Weber, as we saw, moved on the margins of the zone of torrid friendship at the center of which was the poet Stefan George. In a late poem, "Man and Satyr," George has the goat-man sneer, "You are but man . . . our wisdom begins where your wisdom ends." The man replies that the day of myth is over and the Satyr's time is done. Yet, says the Satyr, "it is only through magic that life stays awake." (*Nur durch den Zauber bleibt das Leben wach*). He might not much have liked such teaching, but it is the lesson of Max Weber all the same.

SHORT BIBLIOGRAPHY

Max Weber left many problems to his readers. His most important book, *Economy and Society*, for example, was edited from disordered, fragmentary manuscripts without even the guidance of a plan or table of the proposed contents. It is now available in English in a complete version, well introduced by Guenther Roth and published in three volumes (New York: Bedminster, 1968). But should the reader begin there? I think not. He would do better to tackle *Economy and Society* by way of its parts, in *The City* (Glencoe, Ill.: The Free Press, 1958) or in the quite admirably translated and prefaced volume of essays, *From Max Weber: Essays in Sociology*, edited and translated by H. H. Gerth and C. Wright Mills (New York: Oxford University Press, 1947), which contains much of the best of *Economy and Society*. If he is very strong, however, the beginner might meet the book head-on with the translation of Part I under the title of *The Theory of Social and Economic Organization* (paperback ed., Glencoe, Ill.: The Free Press, 1949), translated by A. M. Henderson and Talcott Parsons. The best preface to that, however, is Parsons' own book, *The Structure of Social Action* (New York: McGraw-

Hill, 1937). That important study is, very reasonably, a massive labor in its own right. So, the essays apart, *Economy and Society* is not the place to begin.

For the reader who comes to Weber by way of religion the situation is easier. In 1930 Parsons' translation of *The Protestant Ethic and the Spirit of Capitalism* (New York: Scribner) was published with an introduction by Richard H. Tawney, whose own *Religion and the Rise of Capitalism* (New York: New American Library, paperback) is still the perfect complement to Weber. (A hostile critique, from the enormous controversy on the *Protestant Ethic*, is Kurt Samuelsson, *Religion and Economic Action* [New York: Basic Books, 1961]. More pious orthodoxies will be found in Shmuel N. Eisenstadt, ed., *The Protestant Ethic, and Modernization: A Comparative View* [New York: Basic Books, 1968].) If the reader is less concerned with the Christian tradition, decent—not more—translations are *The Religion of China: Confucianism and Taoism* (1951), *Ancient Judaism* (1952), *The Religion of India* (1958), all published by The Free Press, Glencoe, Ill. For the most interesting of these, the study of Confucianism and Taoism, articles by O. B. Van Der Sprenkel, "Chinese Religion," *British Journal of Sociology*, V (1954), and "Max Weber on China," *History and Theory*, III (1961) are necessary correctives. The section of *Economy and Society* on *The Sociology of Religion* appeared separately under that title (Boston: Beacon Press, 1964). It is a very barren text. A modern Weberian approach to religion is Michael Hill, *A Sociology of Religion* (London: Allenson, 1973).

Historians may find Weber's *General Economic History*, translated by Frank H. Knight (paperback ed., New York: Macmillan, 1961), interesting, although it is untypical. These lectures are not much as history, but they do show Weber's mind at work both in its generalizing strengths and its weaknesses of structure. More revealing, though it is formally about law and in fact is yet another chunk of *Economy and Society*, is *Max Weber on Law in Economy and Society*, edited by Max Rheinstein and translated by Edward Shils (Cambridge, Mass.: Harvard University Press, 1954). A very simple introduction to Weber's historical sociology of law—and all the better for its simplicity—is Clarence Morris, "Law, Reason and Sociology," *University of Pennsylvania Law Review*, 107 (1958). Marxists ought to have a great deal to say that is of importance about Weber and the interpretation of history. On the whole, however, from Bukharin onward, the Marxists have let us down. Marcuse and Lukács are disappointing on Weber. Perhaps some of the Polish Marxist writers are better, as is claimed, but their books and articles have not been translated. Very useful, in the tradition of historical idealism, is Carlo Antoni, *From History to Sociology: The Transition in German Thinking* (Detroit: Wayne State University Press, 1962). The essays on Troeltsch, Meinecke, and Weber are particularly recommended.

Methodologists and students of the philosophy of the social sciences are well served. If one believes this an important area then, in addition to Runciman's book cited below, there are the tough, well-translated three essays which make up *Max Weber on the Methodology of the Social Sciences*, translated and edited by Edward Shils and Henry A. Finch (Glencoe, Ill.: The Free Press, 1949). Shils's collected papers are about to be published by the University of Chicago Press; all his writings on Weber, too numerous to list here, deserve attention in the same way as do those of Parsons.

There is no full "life and times" of Weber in English. W. Mommsen's book (see below) is specialized and iconoclastic but should be translated. Reinhard Bendix (see below again) gives not so much a portrait as a map, but it is the best map anywhere available of the terrain of Weber's work, and it makes an excellent supplement and companion to the *From Max Weber* volume. These two books are probably, taken together, the irreducible minimum equipment for the English-speaking student of Weber. Practically all that is written on Weber is written in awe. This may be just, but it does get in the way of understanding: when one is knocking one's forehead on the floor one's vision is certainly limited and probably blurred. It is remarkable that despite this awe so much written about Weber is so good, even if so incomplete. The translations, however, are another matter: they are sometimes, as I have tried to note, good, but often they are stilted, difficult, and more obscure than the originals. Nor have all Weber's translators a decent knowledge of English usage. If Weber matters, then much remains to be done by way of both translation and interpretation. Most of all we need a historical sociology of social thought in early twentieth-century Europe such as no writer has yet attempted on a sufficient scale or with sufficient rigor. To say this is not to belittle such a book as H. Stuart Hughes's *Consciousness and Society*, but rather to say that after fifteen years it still stands very much alone. This is a pity for more reasons than the study of Weber, for our century has apparently dedicated itself, only half-knowingly, to acting out the ideas and dreams of these years in deadly earnest. All in all, the writer who in my opinion comes closest to getting the public Weber right was Thomas S. Simey in chapters 4 and 5 of his *Social Science and Social Purpose* (New York: Schocken, 1969), but Lord Simey, alas, did not live to develop his approach in depth.

THE WRITINGS OF MAX WEBER

Zur Geschichte der Handelsgesellschaften im Mittelalter, Nach Sudeuropäischen Quellen (On the History of Medieval Trading Companies, According to Southern European Sources). Stuttgart: F. Enke, 1889.

Die Römische Agrargeschichte in ihrer Bedeutung für das Staats- und Privatrecht. (The Agricultural History of Rome in Its Relation to Public and Private Law). Stuttgart: F. Enke, 1891.

Die Verhältnisse der Landarbeiter im ostelbischen Deutschland (The Conditions of Rural Labour in Germany beyond the Elbe). Vol. 55, *Schriften des Vereins für Sozialpolitik*. Berlin: Duncker & Humblot, 1892.

Gesammelte Aufsätze zur Religionssoziologie (Collected Papers on the Sociology of Religion). 3 vols. Tübingen: J. C. B. Mohr, 1920–1921.

Gesammelte politische Schriften (Collected Political Writings). Munich: Drei Masken Verlag, 1921.

Gesammelte Aufsätze zur Sozial- und Wirtschaftsgeschichte (*Collected Papers on Social and Economic History*). Tübingen: J. C. B. Mohr, 1924.

Gesammelte Aufsätze zur Soziologie und Sozialpolitik (*Collected Papers on Sociology and Social Policy*). Tübingen: J. C. B. Mohr, 1924.

Wirtschaftsgeschichte. Munich: Duncker & Humblot, 1924. English trans: *General Economic History*, S. Hellman and M. Palyi, eds.; Frank H. Knight, trans. London: Collier Macmillan, 1961.

(In subsequent critical editions, the pagination of the original German editions of the posthumous collections has been maintained.)

SOME BOOKS ON WEBER AND HIS TIME

Aron, Raymond. *La Sociologie Allemande Contemporaine.* Paris: Alcan, 1936. New ed., Paris: Presse Universitaire de France, 1966. English trans.: *German Sociology*, Mary and Thomas Bottomore, trans. London: Heinemann, 1957.

Baumgarten, E. *Max Weber, Werk und Person.* Tübingen: J. C. B. Mohr, 1963.

Bendix, Reinhard. *Max Weber: An Intellectual Portrait.* Rev. paperback ed., New York: Doubleday Anchor, 1962.

Brock, Werner. *An Introduction to Contemporary German Philosophy.* Cambridge: Cambridge University Press, 1935.

Dronberger, Ilse. *The Political Thought of Max Weber: In Quest of Statesmanship.* New York: Appleton-Century-Crofts, 1971.

Freund, Julien. *La Sociologie de Max Weber.* Paris: Presses Universitaires de France, 1966. English trans.: *The Sociology of Max Weber*, Mary Ilford, trans. London: Allen Lane. The Penguin Press, 1968.

Honigsheim, Paul. *On Max Weber.* New York: The Free Press, 1968.

Hughes, H. Stuart. *Consciousness and Society: The Reorientation of European Social Thought, 1890–1930.* New York: Harper & Row, 1958.

Loewenstein, Karl. *Max Webers staatspolitische Auffassungen in der Sicht unserer Zeit.* Frankfurt am Main: Athenäum Verlag, 1965. English trans.: *Max Weber's Political Ideas in the Perspective of Our Time.* Amherst: University of Massachusetts Press, 1966.

Mitzman, Arthur. *The Iron Cage: An Historical Interpretation of Max Weber.* New York: Alfred A. Knopf, 1970.

Mommsen, W. *Max Weber und die deutsche Politik, 1890–1920.* Tübingen: J. C. B. Mohr, 1959.

Runciman, Walter G. *A Critique of Max Weber's Philosophy of Social Science.* Cambridge: Cambridge University Press, 1972.

Weber, Marianne. *Max Weber: Ein Lebensbild (Max Weber: A Portrait).* Tübingen: J. C. B. Mohr, 1926.

Weinreich, M. *Max Weber. L'homme et le savant: Etude sur ses idées directrices.* Paris: Vrin, 1938.

INDEX